ELIJAH'S
VICTORY

ELIJAH'S VICTORY

PART 1

Overcoming Evil in Our World

PASTOR JAMES McCLURG

Elijah's Victory, Part 1: Overcoming Evil in Our World
A Bible Teaching Series by Pastor James McClurg

Copyright 2025 by Jambooks
All Rights Reserved Worldwide
ISBN: 978-0-6454298-2-4

This book, or parts thereof, is freely available for sermon material or church or personal Bible study, with acknowledgement of the author, as and where appropriate.

However, the contents of this book, except for the fair use clause above, may not be reproduced or altered, offered for sale, stored in a retrieval system, or transmitted in any form or by any means–electronic, mechanical, photocopying, recording or otherwise, without the prior written permission of the author, subject to Australian copyright law.

Scripture quotations, unless indicated otherwise in the text, are from the New King James (NKJV) Version®. Copyright © 1982 by Thomas Nelson. Used by permission. All rights reserved.

Scripture quotations marked (NIV), are from The Holy Bible, New International Version®, NIV® Copyright © 1973, 1978, 1984, 2011 by Biblica, Inc.®. Used by permission. All rights reserved worldwide.

Scripture quotations marked (NLT) are taken from the *Holy Bible*, New Living Translation, copyright © 1996, 2004, 2015 by Tyndale House Foundation. Used by permission of Tyndale House Publishers, Inc., Carol Stream, Illinois 60188. All rights reserved.

All Greek or Hebrew words with their English meanings in this document, unless indicated otherwise in the text, are sourced from The Exhaustive Concordance of The Bible by James Strong; accessed from the website biblehub.com/strongs.htm at various times during 2022, 2023 and 2024 calendar years.

While the author has made every effort to supply correct website addresses at the time of publication, no responsibility is assumed by the author for errors, or changes that occur after publication.

Further, the author does not have any control over and does not assume any responsibility for third-party websites or their content referred to in this publication. Nor does the author endorse any third-party websites, their authors, or their contents, mentioned in this publication.

For more information about the author or other books available, please visit my website: **jamesmcclurg.com.au**

Contents

Purpose of this Bible Teaching Series 1
Introduction 3

LESSON 1
God Prepares the Way 9

LESSON 2
Words from God Can Be Abrupt 17

LESSON 3
God's Work, Not Our Spirituality 23

LESSON 4
God Breaks Religious Rules 31

LESSON 5
When Life Becomes Uncomfortable 43

LESSON 6
God's Plan Before Our Life Changes 51

LESSON 7
God Provides in Unexpected Ways 59

LESSON 8
God Helps Those With Weak Faith 69

LESSON 9
God Provides Our Daily Bread 83

LESSON 10
First Human Reaction to a Crisis 91

LESSON 11
Second Human Reaction to a Crisis 101

LESSON 12
Honest Prayer 109

LESSON 13
Knowing God and His Blessings 117

A Final Word 125
References 127
Other Books by Pastor James McClurg 129
About the Author 131

Acknowledgments

I wish to thank the following people who assisted in the preparation of this document:

My wife Anthea, for encouraging me to complete the manuscript and publish the book, and for surrendering the many hours spent preparing and writing this material.

Those from Living Word Church, Bundaberg, Queensland, Australia, who patiently attended meetings when I taught an earlier draft of the material in this book.

Pastor H.B. Cruz, Senior Minister, Powerhouse Christian Church, Gold Coast, Queensland, Australia, for helpful suggestions on the title and content of this book.

Patricia Marshall and staff from Luminare Press for editing and preparing the manuscript for publication, including cover design.

Foreword

I have been blessed by the friendship of Pastor James McClurg. He is a faithful intercessor and a skilled expositor of biblical truths. Many have benefited from his teaching which applies God's Word to everyday situations. His long service as a senior pastor has equipped him with valuable insights and expertise to elaborate on the life of Elijah.

Pastor James reveals in this book how Elijah learnt to trust God and obey His voice, even when it meant breaking the religious rules of his time and eating food brought by an unclean bird. This book also explains how Elijah dealt with his emotions and doubts, and how God sustained him with supernatural provision.

This new book from Pastor James is not only informative, but also inspiring and practical. It will help you to live a godly life in any situation. You will enjoy reading this book, as it is written in a clear, engaging style.

Pastor Dallas Hobbs
Pastor, Bundaberg Living Word Church, Queensland
Director, Connexions Ltd., Australia

I have had the pleasure to call James my friend for over forty years, and it is with great pleasure I write this foreword for his new book. Within the pages of this book you will find a tapestry of spiritual teachings. James has the rare gift of distilling complex spiritual concepts into simple, practical guidance that can be applied to our daily lives.

May this book be a source of inspiration, reflection, and transformation. Take your time with it, savour its words, and allow them to become a part of your own spiritual journey. James has gifted us with a treasure in these pages. I hope you find it as enriching and enlightening as I have.

In closing, let us remember the words of Psalm 119:105, "Your word is a lamp to my feet and a light to my path." Let this book serve as a lamp, illuminating your path and reminding you of God's unending grace.

With heartfelt blessings,

Pastor H.B. Cruz
Senior Minister
Powerhouse Christian Church, Gold Coast, Queensland.

"So Ahab sent for all the children of Israel and gathered the prophets together on Mount Carmel. And Elijah came to all the people, and said, 'How long will you falter between two opinions? If the LORD is God, follow Him; but if Baal, follow him.' But the people answered him not a word."

(1 Kings 18:20, 21)

"And it came to pass, at the time of the offering of the evening sacrifice, that Elijah the prophet came near and said, 'LORD God of Abraham, Isaac, and Israel, let it be known this day that You are God in Israel, and I am Your servant, and that I have done all these things at Your word. Hear me, O LORD, hear me, that this people may know that You are the LORD God, and that You have turned their hearts back to You again.'"

(1 Kings 18:36, 37)

"Elijah was a man with a nature like ours, and he prayed earnestly that it would not rain; and it did not rain on the land for three years and six months. And he prayed again, and the heaven gave rain, and the earth produced its fruit."

(James 5:17, 18)

Purpose of this Bible Teaching Series

We in the twenty-first-century church must allow God to teach us spiritual lessons if we are to grow in our Christian lives. These spiritual lessons, I believe, are the same as God taught the prophet Elijah recorded in the Bible in 1 Kings chapter 17. As we learn these lessons, we can begin to fulfill our God-given potential to share His love with all humanity.

Elijah was able to challenge and defeat the evil in his day. God also expects us to successfully challenge and defeat the evil so prevalent in our world today. We can only achieve this with God's strength as we learn these spiritual lessons.

The teaching of this Bible series provides some practical instructions on how to apply these lessons to our daily Christian lives.

There is a short section labelled Personal Application following the teaching from each lesson. If you carefully read each section and apply what you learn to your daily life, you will continue your journey of preparation for wherever God may lead you.

Pastor James McClurg

Pastor James McClurg, November 2023

Introduction

"To the question, 'Where is the God of Elijah?' we answer, 'Where He has always been—on the throne!' But where are the Elijahs of God? We know Elijah was a man of like passions as we are, but alas we are not men of like prayer as he was. One praying man stands as a majority with God! Today God is bypassing men—not because they are too ignorant, but because they are too self-sufficient. Brethren, our abilities are our handicaps, and our talents are our stumbling blocks!"[1]

There are many books, internet sermons, and notes by great authors or teachers on the life of the prophet Elijah as recorded in the Bible. These books, sermons, and notes are available online or at Christian bookstores. You should read, watch, or listen to these when you have the opportunity.

The words in this book explain practical lessons for our Christian life in the twenty-first century, based on the life of Elijah as recorded in 1 Kings chapter 17. These lessons are based on insights God has given me, taught me, or which I have learnt, many times the hard way, by experience.

---

1. Paragraph quoted from "Where are the Elijahs of God?" Sermon classic by Leonard Ravenhill (downloaded from Oneplace.com, 6th May 2022). The word man or men in this paragraph is a generic term meaning men and women.

The text in this manuscript does not come directly from any book or sermon you may read, listen to, or watch, although you may find similar teachings in some material available.

We must read and learn from the whole Bible to be thoroughly equipped for the work God has called us to do. This includes the Old and New Testaments.

"All Scripture is given by inspiration of God, and is profitable for doctrine, for reproof, for correction, for[2] instruction in righteousness, that the man of God may be complete, thoroughly equipped for every good work" (2 Timothy 3:16, 17).

If you have not realized the similarity between the stories of Elijah in 1 Kings chapter 17 and Paul in the New Testament, I pray that you do after reading this book.

Elijah is introduced in the Bible narrative with no listed genealogy. We are informed he was from Gilead. When the promised land was divided by lot in the time of Joshua, the tribes of Reuben, Gad, and half of Manasseh (through his firstborn son Machir) were given land on the east side of the Jordan River. This fulfilled their request to Moses in Numbers chapter 32, which included the land of Gilead (Joshua chapters 13 and 17).

The Bible does not reveal to us which of these tribes Elijah belonged to.

When Jesus found Philip He said to him, "Follow me" (John 1:43). Philip then found Nathanael and told him, "We have found Jesus of Nazareth, the one who Moses in the law and the prophets wrote about" (John 1:45). Nathanael's response was to ask a question, "Can anything good come out of Nazareth?" (John 1:46). Philip challenged Nathanael to come and see for himself.

---

2. Training, discipline (footnote in the NKJV Bible).

Introduction

The inference in Nathanael's question was Nazareth had the reputation as the place where unimportant people lived in the society of his day. He believed nobody who was important in the nation, or their religious system, could come from Nazareth.

God can use anybody to achieve His purposes, regardless of where they come from, their race, age, financial resources, education level, or social standing.

Elijah was chosen by God to destroy the false prophets the evil king and queen had allowed to flourish in the land of Israel. God's plan was to turn the hearts of the people back to Himself.

We need to know without any doubt that God has our world in His control, despite what we see, hear, or read in the news media. God has a plan for our lives and this world, and it will ultimately result in the final defeat of all that is evil.

No devil in hell or any demonic power can ever defeat God's plan. We need to grasp this in our day, just as Elijah had learnt in his preparation for the final defeat of the evil in his day.

Elijah pronounced a one-sentence prophecy to the king, then departed to live by a brook (or creek). There were no more prophecies for the first year. Then he travelled to Zarephath. Elijah had no prophetic word for anybody for the second or third years (except for the widow). Then nothing until halfway through the fourth year. A one-sentence prophecy with nothing more for three and a half years is not exactly a demanding workload.

How would you react if you were in a similar situation to Elijah? "God, why have you forgotten me? I need to be out there preaching your Word, with signs following and prophetic utterances that will change people lives, instead of being stuck here in obscurity."

God had not forgotten Elijah; He was preparing him to change the nation. When it appears to you nothing is happening in your church or ministry, God has not forgotten you either—He is preparing you for your future ministry.

Elijah announced to the evil king and his officials there would be a drought in the land, as God's judgement for their Baal worship and belief in false prophets. The drought lasted for three and a half years.

This timeframe wasn't by accident.

Elijah was not wasting his time during the drought, just counting the days until it was time to confront the prophets of Baal and call down the fire of God. He was learning spiritual lessons to prepare for the final confrontation with the evil in the society of his day.

We must also learn our spiritual lessons from God before we can successfully confront the evil in our day.

God supernaturally supplied food, water, and shelter for Elijah while he was not living among his own people, the Jews. He was staying with a widow from Zarephath, a gentile city. This reveals to me that God provides for anyone who comes to Him by faith in Jesus Christ's death and resurrection, regardless of race or skin colour.

Elijah's story in the Bible provides an answer to two important questions: "Why doesn't God judge evil people?" and "Why do bad things happen on the earth?" God always deals with evil people, no matter who they are. He will restore righteousness and justice to people on this earth. One day He will put an end to all the evil and suffering we see in our world. Jesus Christ will return to this planet to reign in righteousness by His awesome power and authority.

Introduction

May you learn the spiritual lessons Elijah learnt in 1 Kings chapter 17 and be challenged to defeat the evil in your world, as I was challenged as I prepared the material in this book.

LESSON 1

God Prepares the Way

And Elijah the Tishbite, of the inhabitants of Gilead, said to Ahab, "As the LORD God of Israel lives, before whom I stand, there shall not be dew nor rain these years, except at my word." (1 Kings 17:1)

How could Elijah confront Ahab, the evil king of Israel?

He marched right into the palace, into the room where the king made decisions about running the country, past the guards, soldiers, and government officials. Elijah made the announcement, then safely left the building before they could arrest him.

How could did he do it?

Elijah spoke to the evil king because God asked him to. God prepared the way for him to enter the palace and safely depart because he was obedient.

Imagine if God told you to travel to Canberra on the next available airplane and confront the Prime Minister of Australia with the words, "Thus says the Lord…". You must walk past the visitor sign-in desk, security guards, reception desks, locked doors, locked elevators, and security cameras. Then interrupt an important meeting before leaving the building without getting arrested as a terrorist or mentally disturbed person.

How could you do this?

If God did not send you and prepare the way, you would get arrested and likely end up in prison.

When your decisions in life are based on what God has told you to do, not on what you have read, researched, or what others have told you to do, then He will provide and prepare the way for you.

> **You and I must know without any doubt that all our activities are what God wants us to do—our plans, our church or Christian pursuits, and the people we meet or pray with. Then trust God to prepare the way for us.**

The Bible, in the book of Exodus, teaches us God has promised to send His angel before us to prepare the way to do His work on this earth.

"Behold, I send an Angel before you to keep you in the way and to bring you into the place which I have prepared. Beware of Him and obey His voice; do not provoke Him, for He will not pardon your transgressions; for My name is in Him. But if you indeed obey His voice and do all that I speak, then I will be an enemy to your enemies and an adversary to your adversaries. For My Angel will go before you and bring you in to the Amorites and the Hittites and

God Prepares the Way

the Perizzites and the Canaanites and the Hivites and the Jebusites; and I will[3] cut them off" (Exodus 23:20-23).

Paul, in the book of Ephesians, teaches us that we are unwise if we are not careful how we live. "Be very careful, then, how you live—not as unwise but as wise, making the most of every opportunity, because the days are evil. Therefore do not be foolish, but understand what the Lord's will is. Do not get drunk on wine, which leads to debauchery. Instead, be filled with the Spirit," (Ephesians 5:15-18, NIV).

If you or I do not know God's will we are foolish, according to Paul in the verses above.

Paul reminds us to be strong in the Lord: "Finally, my brethren, be strong in the Lord and in the power of His might" (Ephesians 6:10).

The word 'finally' comes before instructions about putting on the whole armour of God to be able to stand against the schemes or plans of the devil (verses 11-18). This word, 'finally,' also comes after chapters 1 to 5. In these chapters, Paul gives us teachings on walking with God, who we are in Him, understanding God's will, and navigating relationships with family, work, church, finances, and prayer.

Unless we live the way God wants us to by making these relationships right, as best we can, we will never fully succeed in our Christian life as God intended, even if we put on all of God's armour.

Elijah knew the still, small voice of God. In 1 Kings 19:11-13, God instructed Elijah to stand on the mountain before the LORD. When the LORD passed by Elijah, there was a violent wind, followed by a powerful earthquake, then

---

3. Annihilate them (footnote in the NKJV Bible).

a mighty fire. Elijah recognised the still, small voice of God following all these physical and spiritual manifestations.

We must hear God's voice to understand His will. His voice is never associated with great physical or spiritual occurrences.

> **Mighty demonstrations of God's miraculous power are associated with His presence, but His guiding voice is always soft and gentle.**

Jesus taught about the shepherd with his sheep in John 10:1-16. He taught that He was the Good Shepherd, and His sheep know His voice.

Learning to know God's voice is another lesson series. There are plenty of teaching series on this. I am sure you can find some to learn how you can hear and obey God's voice.

When we are obedient to God's voice we will have stability in our daily lives, despite the confusion so prevalent in our world today. God will use our stability to draw others to Himself. This should be our primary purpose for each day we are alive on the planet.

If you do not obey God's still, small voice, you will never have stability in your Christian life. You will be unsure, indecisive, and easily swayed by other people's opinions, especially when they disagree with your actions. Your faith will be tested when people question your motives, especially those from your own church, fellowship, or denomination.

One of the churches my wife and I pastored was in an area where some of the local Christian churches had endured church splits. Many Christian people were disillusioned with church infighting causing tensions between family members and close friends.

Our church never achieved large attendance numbers, even though we were there a few years.

Our ministry was to teach Christian people not to abandon their faith. Some people we ministered to came to our church, some did not. Once they were strong enough in God, some people attending our church returned to the church they had come from.

Some ministers criticized and judged us because our church was different from others. We were not pastoring a growing church (in terms of numbers attending) with great programs and facilities as they thought we were supposed to do.

We were doing what God called us to do. He always prepared the way for us regardless of what other ministers thought or said.

I was travelling through that district a few years after we had left. The song leader in a larger Pentecostal church I attended on Sunday morning was one of the guys we helped to overcome the difficulties in his life while he attended our church. This was a great encouragement for us, to know we had made a difference in someone else's life during our time pastoring that church.

True Christian spirituality is to do what God wants you to do because you have obeyed His voice, then trusting Him to prepare the way regardless of what others say about you. This is more important, I believe in God's eyes, than any church activities, programs, or ministries you may be involved in.

Jesus taught us to pray in what is commonly known as the Lord's Prayer, recorded in Matthew 6:8–13 (part of the

Sermon on the Mount) and Luke 11:2–4. The last part of the prayer includes these words, "And do not lead us into temptation, but deliver us from the evil one."

If seeking His kingdom is the focus of my prayer, not my kingdom, then I can overcome temptation by prayer. Nothing the devil can tempt me with is worth it compared to what God has already promised me. God will always prepare the way and provide for me to do His will.

The devil can't tempt me to think God has overlooked or forgotten me because I know God has never forgotten me and will never forsake me. God has promised my daily bread. What more do I need?

The devil can't tempt me to do whatever I can to increase my bank account because God has promised to provide for me. The devil can't tempt me to steal something because God promised I will never be begging bread.

The devil can't tempt me with a new colour TV that is bigger and clearer than the one I have. Why do I need it?

If we focus on God's kingdom first, then we will have a different mindset or motivation for what we do than everyone else we associate with who doesn't know God as we do. We will be living on another level compared to those who are not perceiving things from God's perceptive. People will be coming to us for the answers to the problems in their world.

- ❑ That's when the reputation of the church will be what it is meant to be, as God desires it to be.
- ❑ That's when our families will be what they are supposed to be.

God Prepares the Way

- ❏ That's when our society will be what God intended it to be, instead of the mess that it is now.
- ❏ That's when God's revival will come to our land.

So, the challenge I want you to consider from this lesson is threefold:

1. Are you sure you are doing what God wants you to do?
2. What is your prayer life like?
3. Is our Lord's Prayer the pattern of your prayer?

God is looking for people who have stability in their lives because of their faith in Him and His provision. The world is looking for people who have this stability. How do you and I measure up today?

Personal Application

Examine all your church and personal Christian activities you do in the light of the discussion above. Answer the following questions as honestly as you can:

1. Are you sure the activities in your life are what God told you to do, or are they based on what others told you, on what your denomination or group expects you to do, or what you thought was a great idea?

2. Do you know the soft and gentle voice of God? Are you obedient to His voice?

3. How do you cope with criticism from others, especially if they are from your own church, congregation, or denominational group?

4. Do you have stability in your life based on the Lord's Prayer?

After reading the discussion above, are there any changes to your life or ministry you need to make?

LESSON 2

Words from God Can Be Abrupt

And Elijah the Tishbite, of the inhabitants of Gilead, said to Ahab, "As the LORD God of Israel lives, before whom I stand, there shall not be dew nor rain these years, except at my word." (1 Kings 17:1)

This prophecy of Elijah is one of the shortest in the whole Bible. It was also one of the most effective, like a devastating hand grenade.

Elijah proclaimed a single sentence that confronted the false religion introduced into the land of Israel by the evil King Ahab and his wife Jezebel.

I attended a church meeting where a young girl about seven or eight years old gave a wonderful prophecy. It was brief. She used the language of a child she was familiar with, without any large theological words or King James Language Bible references. Everybody present knew this was a word directly from the throne of God.

> A word from God can be abrupt. Its importance is not determined by its length, language, scriptural references quoted, or even the volume or mannerisms of the speaker.

There are four parts to Elijah's prophecy. Each is discussed below.

1) As the LORD God of Israel lives

No one had dared to use the name of the LORD God of Israel, publicly at least, when Ahab and Jezebel were ruling God's people. Anyone who did so was risking death. Obadiah hid, fed, and looked after 100 prophets of the LORD while Jezebel killed all the other prophets in the land (1 Kings 18:13).

Elijah used the name of the LORD God of Israel right at the throne or the place of power in the land. His prophecy challenged the authority and power of the false prophets who were ruling the land.

David said similar words when he confronted Goliath many years before Elijah's time (1 Samuel 17:45–47). When Moses and Aaron confronted Pharaoh and the false prophets (wise men, sorcerers, soothsayers, or magicians) of Egypt, they did so in the name of the LORD, the God of the Hebrew slaves (Exodus chapters 7 to 12).

The false prophets used demonic (or occult, black magic) power to copy the first miraculous sign of Moses and Aaron—the rod that became a snake. They also copied the first two plagues—the water that became blood, and the plague of frogs. The false prophets could not copy any of the other eight supernatural signs or plagues God delivered after Moses warned Pharaoh. Two out of ten is a failure in anyone's language.

I read in the Gospels Jesus gave the demonic powers permission to leave (Luke 8:32, 33). He was always in control, even over demon-possessed people.

Elijah spoke the words, "As the LORD God of Israel *lives.*" This proclamation in these first seven words of his prophecy was a daring statement that the God of Israel was still alive. This proved to Jezebel that even though she thought she had destroyed any memory of the God of Israel when she killed all the LORD's prophets, she was wrong.

You or I may not have seen Him lately, but we need to know the LORD God of Israel is still alive and in control of our world today. The world as we know it is not out of control, despite what we read or hear in the news media. It is exactly where God wants it to be before the glorious day when He will return to this earth.

God is still in control of everything that happens in or to our lives, our families, or our friends. That is a wonderful thought to meditate on as we consider this prophecy of Elijah from 1 Kings chapter 17.

2) Before whom I stand (whom I serve, NIV)

Elijah proclaimed he was a servant of the God of Israel. He was not afraid to declare whom he served. This was his whole motivation for being on planet Earth.

If we are doing God's will, there is nothing the devil or life on this planet can throw at us that cannot be defeated by the power within us (1 John 4:1–4).

We have the same strength, power, and ability Elijah had. "But if the Spirit of Him who raised Jesus from the dead dwells in you, He who raised Christ from the dead will also give life to your mortal bodies[4] through His Spirit who dwells in you" (Romans 8:11).

I can face today and every tomorrow because He lives within my heart. I am confident to defeat all the works of the devil because Jesus's power lives in me. That same power lives in you, so you should have this same confidence.

3) The weather forecast—there shall not be dew nor rain these years

God was saying through the words of Elijah, "This will test if Baal is god or not. You ask your god to bring the rain and sun to guarantee the crops. Baal is supposed to be the god of fertility and abundance. Let us see how he handles not having any rain for a while."

Elijah's prophetic sentence reminded the people that the sunshine and rain that helped their crops and livestock flourish came from the God of Israel, not from Baal.

It was God's weather forecast, not Elijah's.

Any prophecy or word from the Lord must be consistent with God's Word, the Bible. If any word or prophecy is not consistent with what the Bible teaches, it is not from God.

"I marvel that you are turning away so soon from Him who called you in the grace of Christ, to a different gospel, which is not another; but there are some who trouble you and want to pervert[5] the gospel of Christ. But even if we, or an angel from heaven, preach any other gospel to you than what we have preached to you, let him be[6] accursed. As we have said before, so now I say again, if anyone preaches any

---

4. Or because of (footnote in the NKJV Bible).
5. Distort (footnote in the NKJV Bible).
6. Greek, anathema (footnote in the NKJV Bible).

other gospel to you than what you have received, let him be accursed" (Galatians 1:6–9).

"This is how you can recognize the Spirit of God: Every spirit that acknowledges that Jesus Christ has come in the flesh is from God, but every spirit that does not acknowledge Jesus is not from God. This is the spirit of the antichrist, which you have heard is coming and even now is already in the world" (1 John 4:2, 3, NIV).

The God of Israel sends rain when the people of the land follow Him but withholds rain when they do not (Deuteronomy 11:13–17).

So often we focus on or talk about the good things God does—His love, mercy, and forgiveness. Sometimes we forget He also has pronounced trouble or curses on people who forsake or leave Him out of their lives (Deuteronomy 28:15–68). One of these curses can be drought on the land resulting in famine.

4) The last part of his weather forecast—except at my word.

What incredible faith Elijah had in His God and His Word.

Elijah knew without any doubt God would do exactly what He said He would do, because he had already learnt Lesson 1. He knew he was proclaiming what God wanted him to.

James 5:17, 18 teaches us Elijah was a man like you and me. Therefore, we can have the same faith in God and His Word as Elijah displayed.

We can do what Elijah did! Absolutely. We can turn our workplaces, our families, and our communities back to God.

Personal Application

Do YOU believe YOU can overcome all the power of the evil one? If you do, how do you react to the difficulties in your life, family, or church?

Have you the same faith in God's Word as Elijah had? Consider the following scriptures as you honestly answer this question:

- Matthew chapter 6, especially verses 8 and 25–34.
- Philippians 4, especially verses 6, 7, 13, and 19.
- James 5:17, 18

Try memorising any of the verses listed above that apply to your personal situation.

LESSON 3

God's Work, Not Our Spirituality

Then the word of the LORD came to him, saying, "Get away from here and turn eastward, and hide by the Brook Cherith, which flows into the Jordan"...So he went and did according to the word of the LORD, for he went and stayed by the Brook Cherith, which flows into the Jordan. (1 Kings 17:2, 3, 5)

Elijah obeyed the word of the LORD to stay or hide in the brook. The English word 'hide' in verse 3 is translated from the Hebrew word '*sathar*,' which has an English meaning of 'be absent, keep close, conceal, hide self, keep secret, surely.'

In verse 5, the English word 'stayed' is translated from the Hebrew word '*yashab*,' which has an English meaning of 'to sit, remain, dwell'.

There is no indication in the Hebrew that Elijah was hiding, running away in fear of his life, expecting soldiers sent by the evil king to appear at any moment ready to kill him. Any inference in these verses that Elijah was afraid reveals the challenge of translating the Hebrew into English so we can understand what we read.

The evil King Ahab and his queen Jezebel would have had Elijah killed if he did not obey God by staying by the brook. They were out looking for him because they blamed him for the drought in the land. They did not examine themselves or realise they were responsible for the drought because of their evil deeds.

There are many examples in Bible times and our day of people who blame God when things go wrong in their lives instead of examining themselves to see what they need to change. The result is always hardship and evil in their own lives and/or family.

One biblical example is the story of Cain and Abel. Cain became angry at God and his brother Abel because God did not respect or accept his offering (Genesis 4:2–8). He murdered his brother instead of examining his own life to change what was needed so that God would also respect or accept his offering.

There was a lady in a church we pastored who received a word from the Lord that God would provide a better job for her in His time. So, she quit her job that very week.

Then, instead of waiting for His timing or examining why she left her job when she did, she blamed God, us, and everyone else she could because God did not immediately provide a better job for her. She had difficulty in trusting God's faithfulness from then on in her Christian life.

God had given Elijah control over the weather. That was awesome authority from the Lord!

God's Work, Not Our Spirituality

He did not appear in public proclaiming to everybody how God had given him such power and authority. If he had done so, the soldiers sent by the evil king would have executed him.

Instead, Elijah hid or lived by the brook and God kept him safe from Ahab, Jezebel and their soldiers. He stayed where he was until God told him it was time to move, even though he had delivered a powerful message from God to Ahab.

I have watched a documentary on the life of Billy Graham, the great American Evangelist (released 2018 by Billy Graham Evangelistic Films). In the documentary, Billy said "God's work was always about the message, never about the messenger."

> **God's work is never dependent on our ability, talents, Bible knowledge, or what we have done for Him.**

- ❑ If you or I try to live our Christian life by our own strength, natural ability, or academic learning, we will fail.

- ❑ If you or I think our prayers, our words of knowledge, or counsel are more important or spiritual than what someone else may pray or say, we will fail.

- ❑ If you or I think we are above everyone else in our knowledge of spiritual things or in our spiritual power or spiritual gifts, we will fail.

- ❑ If you or I think we have the greatest Bible knowledge to answer or refute all those who are sceptics, we will fail.

- ❑ Eventually, we will come across someone who has greater Bible knowledge than we do, or who will ask us questions we cannot answer.

However, if you or I rely on the Spirit of God, no one will be able to answer Him speaking through us. That is what happened to Stephen as recorded in the following verses:

"And Stephen, full of[7] faith and power, did great wonders and signs among the people. Then there arose some from what is called the Synagogue of the Freedmen (Cyrenians, Alexandrians, and those from Cilicia and Asia), disputing with Stephen. *And they were not able to resist the wisdom and the Spirit by which he spoke*" (Acts 6:8–10, emphasis added).

Jesus appeared to Saul in the miraculous way he was converted, healed of blindness, baptised in water, and received the Holy Spirit (read Acts 9:1–19). Saul, who later became the apostle Paul, immediately preached Jesus as the Messiah in the synagogues of Damascus (verse 20).

The Jews in Damascus wanted to kill him because of what he was now preaching in their synagogues. He escaped by night and fled to Jerusalem, in fear of his very life (Acts 9:23–25).

In Jerusalem, the disciples were afraid of Paul until Barnabas brought him to them (Acts 9:26, 27). Paul preached about Jesus to the Jews in Jerusalem, but they also tried to kill him. The disciples sent him to Caesarea and then to

---

7. Grace (footnote in the NKJV Bible).

Tarsus (his hometown) to keep him safe from the threats of the Jews (Acts 9:29, 30).

In Galatians chapters 1 and 2, Paul reveals some details on what happened after the events recorded in Acts chapter 9. Three years after his conversion he travelled to Arabia, Damascus, Syria, Cilicia, and Jerusalem, where he stayed with Peter and James for fifteen days.

Apart from this trip he was out of the spotlight, living in his hometown of Tarsus for fourteen years. That is a long time in the wilderness. Many of the Christian people of that day only heard the rumours that Saul, who spent so much of his life trying to destroy God's church, was now converted and preaching the faith he had once tried to destroy.

Paul tells us more in Acts 22:17–21 (NIV):

> When I returned to Jerusalem and was praying at the temple, I fell into a trance and saw the Lord speaking to me. "Quick!" he said. "Leave Jerusalem immediately, because the people here will not accept your testimony about me."
>
> "Lord," I replied, "these people know that I went from one synagogue to another to imprison and beat those who believe in you. And when the blood of your martyr[8] Stephen was shed, I stood there giving my approval and guarding the clothes of those who were killing him."
>
> Then the Lord said to me, "Go; I will send you far away to the Gentiles."

---

8. Or witness (footnote in the NIV Bible)

Paul had a great testimony God could have used to turn the world upside down for His glory. Instead, he argued with God.

What he was saying, in my words, was: "Don't you see the revival I could bring for you Lord? I could really take your message now. My talents, life story, and knowledge of the Jewish religious law, could be used so much for your kingdom to refute everyone who opposed you as I did."

Paul could never fulfill God's calling on his life until he hid himself in Tarsus where he learnt lessons about the grace of God, practical Christian living, and spiritual warfare. These lessons he teaches us in his many letters found in the New Testament.

I pray that you can understand the similarity between the life of Elijah in 1 Kings 17 and that of Paul in the New Testament.

The prophet Samuel anointed David as king to replace Saul (1 Samuel 16:13). When King Saul sent for David, he was still looking after the sheep, even though he had the power of the Holy Spirit upon him (1 Samuel 16:17–19).

David knew the power of his God would defeat the Philistine giant Goliath because he had killed the lion and the bear when they tried to take one of his sheep (1 Samuel 17:34–36). When King Saul questioned his ability to face Goliath, David told the king, "'The LORD, who delivered me from the paw of the lion and from the paw of the bear, He will deliver me from the hand of this Philistine'" (1 Samuel 17:37).

God was preparing David to defeat the giant while he was looking after the sheep. I believe David wrote some of the psalms while he was looking after the sheep (for example Psalm 23). David built his relationship with

God's Work, Not Our Spirituality

God during this time in his life, instead of complaining about his situation.

"And when they had performed everything according to the Law of the Lord, they returned into Galilee to their own town of Nazareth. And the child grew and became strong; he was filled with wisdom and the grace of God was on him" (Luke 2:39, 40, NIV, referring to the early life of Jesus Christ).

Luke records in the next verses that Jesus's mum and earthly dad could not find him for three days. When his mum finally found him, she was angry. Jesus did not become angry with them because He had an important job to do or was on a very tight time schedule.

"Then he went down to Nazareth with them and was obedient to them. But his mother treasured all these things in her heart. And Jesus grew in wisdom and in stature, and in favor with God and man" (Luke 2:51, 52, NIV).

> **Elijah, Paul, David, or Jesus himself would never have fulfilled God's plan for their lives if they had relied on their own abilities, learning, or talents.**

You or I cannot either.

Personal Application

- Do you live your Chrisitan life based on your abilities, talents, or Bible knowledge, or do you trust God to use you despite your failings or circumstances?

- Is your testimony about what YOU have done for God, rather than what God has done for or through you?

- Have you ever felt God has abandoned you when you have time away from the spotlight?

- When that happens, do you use the time to allow God to speak to you and strengthen your relationship with Him, or do you complain about what has happened to you?

- What do you need to do to change?

LESSON 4

God Breaks Religious Rules

"And it will be that you shall drink from the brook, and I have commanded the ravens to feed you there." So he went and did according to the word of the LORD, for he went and stayed by the Brook Cherith, which flows into the Jordan. The ravens brought him bread and meat in the morning, and bread and meat in the evening; and he drank from the brook. (1 Kings 17:4-6)

God miraculously supplied Elijah with bread and meat in the wilderness. It was a reminder to Elijah that God supplied bread and meat for the children of Israel in the wilderness (Exodus chapter 16).

This was a direct sign to Elijah, I believe, that the God of the Bible was still in control of his situation. God had not abandoned Elijah. He will never abandon you or me either in our time of need, whatever that need may be (read Matthew 6:25-34).

The Hebrew word, '*oreb*,' translated as the English word 'ravens' in verses 4 and 6 of 1 Kings chapter 17, applies to a species of the crow family, several of which are commonly found in Palestine. The raven resembles the crow but is larger, weighing three pounds (or 1.4 kilograms) and its black colour is more iridescent.[9]

Ravens and crows are scavengers, unclean animals for Jewish people (Leviticus 11:15). I have seen black crows destroy the contents of someone's rubbish bin when they leave the lid off or not closed completely. Would you eat the food the ravens or crows brought for breakfast and dinner every day?

Elijah had to trust God that the provision from the ravens every night for dinner and every morning for breakfast was healthy and clean. He had to overlook the religious rules of what was clean or unclean for him to eat. If he did not, he would have starved.

> **God overrules religious rules, taboos, or prejudices, including racial or economic barriers.**

God loves all people regardless of nationality, skin or hair colour or style, age, economic or marital status, religious affiliation (or no affiliation), or belief system. We must do the same.

It saddens me, and I believe it saddens God, when a Christian or a church judges or discriminates against others based on any of these things (read James 2:1–12).

Every person on the planet has the same basic need—a blessed hope that one day they will meet the God in heaven

---

9. Information in this paragraph sourced from *Bible Names Dictionary, Smith* (1863).

who created the universe. This hope can give all of us a reason for getting out of bed every morning. We all need the salvation that is found only in knowing Jesus Christ as our Lord and Saviour.

"so that *everyone who believes in him* will have eternal life.[10] For this is how God loved the world: He gave[11] his one and only Son, so that *everyone who believes in him* will not perish but have eternal life" (John 3:15, 16, NLT, emphasis added).

"For *all have sinned* and fall short of the glory of God" (Romans 3:23, emphasis added).

Salvation must always produce changes in a person's life. These changes are more than going to church, attending prayer meetings and Bible studies, or telling people about the love of God. Our Christian life must result in continual changes in all we do, including the relationships we maintain with other people, family members, our work, and friends, as well as our attitude toward money.

There will always be people and churches who teach that keeping their religious rules or regulations is more important than simple faith in the death and resurrection of Jesus Christ cleansing us from all sin. We must always refute this religious view with gentleness, respect, love, and the power of the Holy Spirit within us.

> Therefore do not let anyone judge you by what you eat or drink, or with regard to a religious festival, a New Moon celebration or a Sabbath day. These are a shadow of the things that were to come; the reality,

---

10. Or everyone who believes will have eternal life in him (footnote in the NLT Bible).
11. Or For God loved the world so much that he gave (footnote in the NLT Bible).

however, is found in Christ. Do not let anyone who delights in false humility and the worship of angels disqualify you. Such a person also goes into great detail about what they have seen; they are puffed up with idle notions by their unspiritual mind. They have lost connection with the head, from whom the whole body, supported and held together by its ligaments and sinews, grows as God causes it to grow.

Since you died with Christ to the elemental spiritual forces of this world, why, as though you still belonged to the world, do you submit to its rules: 'Do not handle! Do not taste! Do not touch?' These rules, which have to do with things that are all destined to perish with use, are based on merely human commands and teachings. Such regulations indeed have an appearance of wisdom, with their self-imposed worship, their false humility and their harsh treatment of the body, but they lack any value in restraining sensual indulgence. (Colossians 2:16–23, NIV)

When my wife and I were the ministers at a church in North Queensland, Friday nights were devoted to prayer and worship, followed by music practice for the following Sunday morning service. We nearly always practiced two fast songs, followed by two slower songs to allow the congregation to spend a short time worshipping God.

We started the services at 9:30 a.m. Sunday mornings and finished close to or just after 11 a.m. to allow people to leave, if needed, for family reasons.

One Sunday morning service, we had not finished singing the first song when the congregation started to respond

God Breaks Religious Rules

to the presence of God. Some people started laughing softly while some started crying. Others started singing songs we had not practiced for that service.

We had individual plastic chairs for people to use during the service. One man fell onto the floor and scattered some of these chairs. There was no one near him or praying for him. I prayed for many of the congregation who were there that morning.

That Sunday morning at 10:45 a.m. we still hadn't proceeded past the first fast song in the order of service. I closed the meeting. Most people did not want to leave. There were no announcements, offering, communion, or preaching, because God moved upon us.

Had we wasted our time on Friday night learning the other three songs? Did I waste my time preparing a sermon for that Sunday service? Not at all.

The people who attended responded to the presence of God, which was more important than anything that was part of our normal Sunday service or I had prepared for that day.

The religious leaders criticised Jesus's disciples because they did not conform to the traditions of the elders (the religious traditions of the day):

Mark 7:1–5 (NIV) provides one example of the Pharisees criticism.

> The Pharisees and some of the teachers of the law who had come from Jerusalem gathered around Jesus and saw some of his disciples eating food with hands that were defiled, that is, unwashed. (The Pharisees and all the Jews do not eat unless they give their hands a ceremonial washing, holding to the tradition of the elders. When they come from the marketplace

they do not eat unless they wash. And they observe many other traditions, such as the washing of cups, pitchers and kettles.)[12] So the Pharisees and teachers of the law asked Jesus, "Why don't your disciples live according to the tradition of the elders instead of eating their food with defiled hands?"

The topic of controversy in these verses was not proper hygiene, but the Pharisaic lifestyle that made strict standards of ceremonial purity the embodiment of true religion. Unfortunately, by making such behaviour as ritual washings the measure of orthodoxy, these Pharisees not only overlooked, but indeed violated, other areas of God's Word. Jesus set the issue of cleanliness on a new plane (Mark 7:6–23), insisting that sin, not certain foods or other objects, separates a person from fellowship and worship.[13]

One year I attended a church midnight mass on Christmas Eve. Another year I also attended an Easter Sunday service at a different church. Both churches had traditional events with services commemorating the Christmas and Easter biblical stories. There was so much spiritual meaning in the words, hymns, and symbolism within each service.

However, both churches proclaimed the importance of upholding their traditions concerning these events, rather than faith in the birth, death, and resurrection of Jesus Christ setting people free from the power of sin in their lives.

During his time of ministry before his arrest, Jesus deliberately broke many of the rules of the religious leaders of his day:

---

12. Some early manuscripts pitchers, kettles and dining couches (footnote in the NIV Bible).

13. Information in this paragraph is sourced from Asbury Bible Commentary, Carpenter (Editor, 1992)

God Breaks Religious Rules

- He ate with tax collectors and sinners (Matthew 9:9–13)
- He healed people on the Sabbath (for example Luke 14:1–6; John 5:1–14)
- He touched and healed those who had leprosy (Luke 5:12, 13)
- When His disciples plucked grain and ate it on the Sabbath, Jesus revealed to the Pharisees that He was Lord even of the Sabbath (Matthew 12:1–8)

There is one story of the life of Jesus where He and His disciples contravened the bigotry of the religious leaders of His day, which we can read in John chapter 4. It is the story of Jesus going out of his way to minister to a Samaritan woman who was taking water from a well.

Jesus was on his way from Judea to Galilee (verse 3). The shortest route from Jerusalem to Galilee was a high road straight through Samaritan territory. Most Jews would not travel by this road, for they regarded any contact with Samaritans as contaminating their holiness in the God of their fathers.

The words of verse 4, "But He needed to go through Samaria," show an expression of necessity. As the Saviour of all humanity, Jesus felt He had to confront the smouldering suspicion and enmity between Jews and Samaritans by ministering to his enemies.[14]

It was the middle of a hot, dry, dusty day. Jesus and His disciples were tired (or exhausted), hungry, and thirsty from walking all morning. He asked the lady for a drink of water from the well.

---

14. The Expositor's Bible Commentary, Barker and Kohlenberger (2004).

This set the scene for the conversation between Jesus and the Samaritan lady that led to her and many of the people in that city believing that He was the Christ, the Messiah, and the Saviour of the world (verses 7–42).

The disciples had gone into the city to buy food (verse 8). This was a disgusting Samaritan city or village to religious Jewish people of that day. Because their hunger and tiredness were so acute, the disciples had no choice but to overcome any racial and religious bigotry they held toward Samaritans.

> **If we have a hunger for God to move in our lives and churches, we must overcome any racial or religious bigotry or discrimination. We must share the gospel of our Father's love with everyone we encounter.**

When we are motivated to see God's power change people's lives, as He has changed our lives, this becomes more important than what is happening in our own personal or family life. God will often test us on our commitment to this.

While the pastor of a previous church, I arrived home after one Friday night meeting to find that my wife, Anthea, had just received a phone call. Someone we knew had just been admitted to hospital after an accident. I had about two minutes to freshen up and grab my anointing oil before driving to the hospital. God did something good for the person who was in hospital, and I did not finally drive home until well into the early hours of the next morning.

This was after a long week at work (I still had my secular, full-time job). I usually ate dinner then relaxed at home after

God Breaks Religious Rules

the Friday night church meetings. I said to God, "This is not fair because I need Friday night just to relax and clear my mind from working all week before I prepare for Sunday."

God said to me, "No, you don't need that time, I want you to go and do this." I had to obey even though it was very inconvenient.

When the Samaritan lady at the well stopped looking at her own situation, God could touch her life (John 4:28-42). As she walked back into that city, she forgot her inhibitions, social standing, and personal problems. She talked to everyone she met about the man at the well before inviting them to come and see for themselves if He was the Messiah.

The whole city was dramatically changed for the glory of God. Many in that city came to know God personally. Jesus stayed there for two days. That is the revival power of our God at work right there.

Just as Jesus used this opportunity as recorded in John chapter 4, I believe that we all should use every opportunity to share the goodness of God with others, "making the most of every opportunity because the days are evil" (Ephesians 5:16, NIV).

I believe we have divine opportunities every day. What God needs from us is the wisdom to ask for the key or divine revelation for every situation we face. We need to be kind and help people in order to be able to share God's love.

When we see a frustrated driver on the side of the road with their car bonnet up, obviously wondering why the car will not start, what do we do? Instead of driving past like everyone else, or praying, "Thank you Lord that is not me," stop and ask, "I may not be the greatest mechanic, but can I help? Let me give you a lift somewhere. Perhaps I can ring someone for you? Maybe I can help pay for the repairs or the tow truck if needed?" Sounds like the parable of the good Samaritan to me.

What do we do when we see a mother struggling with a small child as she tries to push a trolley full of groceries down the escalator or to her car? Do we just walk by like everyone else, or judge her by thinking to ourselves, "What a silly lady for buying so many groceries all at once?" We should stop and ask, "Can I help you?"

In Acts chapter 10, Cornelius, a Roman soldier in Caesarea, sent three men to Joppa (forty-eight kilometres away), to look for Peter. Some brothers from Joppa and Peter walked with them back to Caesarea to meet Cornelius. Peter went because of a vision God gave him.

Cornelius and many of his friends and soldiers were waiting in Caesarea to hear Peter preach. They were saved, filled with the Holy Spirit, as evidenced by speaking in tongues, and baptised in water.

However, in Acts chapter 11, Peter had to explain his actions to some of the believers in Jerusalem. These believers accused him of breaking the religious laws by entering the house and eating with gentile people (those who were not of their ancestry or religious group). After Peter explained what happened, these believers were satisfied that God had also granted repentance and eternal life to gentiles, just as He had to Jewish people.

In Acts chapter 15, there was a dispute in the church in Antioch about whether gentile people could be saved without keeping the religious rules of the Jewish people (that is, the laws of Moses). The first council of the early church met to consider this question.

After much discussion, James made a judgement, based on scriptural evidence (from our Old Testament), that they should send a letter to the gentile believers. The letter stated no burden should be placed on them (they did not need to fulfill the religious laws of the Jewish people), except to abstain from food offered to idols, sexual immorality, strangled animals, and blood.

I attended a church meeting in a regional city in Coastal Queensland. The Senior Pastor of that church shared his vision for the church to grow to more than double the size that it was at that time (in terms of numbers attending). His church building was in part of the Central Business District. There was a walkway and river at the back of the church property.

When I was talking to him, he was complaining that the local street people used the back of his church as a place to shelter or stay overnight, especially when it rained. Sometimes they would use the back area as a toilet, leaving an awful smell that had to be cleaned before any church meetings. He even boasted the police were on nightly patrols to keep such nuisances away from his clean church premises.

His idea of church growth was middle-income (or above) people with respectable jobs and social standing joining his church. That pastor had no concept that his church was located where it was to enable the homeless or street people in that city to experience God's love.

There are people we meet every day who are waiting for what we have—the love of God reaching out to those in need.

Will we share it?

Personal Application

- Study James 2:1–13. Are there any areas of your life or ministry you need to change after meditating on these verses?

- Do you or your church have religious taboos or rules that you need to change?

- Are you so hungry for the moving of God's supernatural power in your life, ministry, and community that whatever you experience in your life, including any religious taboos or rules, are not important anymore?

- Read again the story at the end of the discussion above, about the pastor of a church in a regional city.

- Is there anything in your Christian life or ministry that you need to ask God to change?

LESSON 5

When Life Becomes Uncomfortable

And it happened after a while that the brook dried up, because there had been no rain in the land.
(1 Kings 17:7)

The brook where Elijah was living dried up. Elijah was quite comfortable by the brook. God supernaturally supplied his food every day and provided him with water to drink. Elijah could live a relaxed lifestyle. He did not have to work or look for food or water to survive the drought.

Have you noticed what happens after heavy rain stops, with no further rain for a prolonged time? The result is the brooks (or creeks) stop flowing. Not overnight, but gradually.

Elijah watched as the water level became lower and the brook flowed more slowly. It finally stopped flowing and dried up. Maybe the water started getting muddy or became stagnant or started to smell.

He could have panicked because the water supply dried up. "Where am I going to get water from in the middle of the drought? How am I going to survive now?"

Elijah did not look for a shovel to dig into the water hole so that he could find enough fresh water to survive. Nor did he walk along the brook to try to find another waterhole that would last longer or was not stagnant or starting to smell. Elijah had to learn to trust that God was still in control, even if his circumstances were changing and he did not understand why God had allowed this to happen.

> **If our lives become unsettled or suddenly change, we need to know if God is leading us to learn more spiritual lessons.**

When our prayers seem to be ineffective or our circumstances change, we need to ask God what He is doing and how or where He is leading us. We must be willing to follow God's way, regardless of what we may think, like, or feel comfortable with. You and I need to learn to trust that God knows what He is doing, even (and especially) if we do not.

I have been the pastor of smallish churches in rural towns or suburbs of regional towns or cities for over thirty-five years. During that time, I also worked full time in a secular job until I started my own business. This allowed me to have time to devote to church work while still supporting my family and myself.

God was wonderfully blessing my business, and I was making a good level of income.

When Life Becomes Uncomfortable

Then an economic crunch came, suddenly and dramatically. My business income dropped 90 percent in less than eighteen months. I was in a desperate financial situation. Praise God my wife still had a job as a full-time primary school teacher, so we had some income to support our family.

I was tempted to start to panic.

It was then that I had to learn to trust God, that He knew where He was leading me and my family, even if I did not understand where God was in the situation.

I knew that our time in the church we had pastored for twenty-one years had now ended, so I applied for secular jobs in my professional capacity. This took a period of just over twelve months. I was finally offered a position in another Queensland coastal city, which resulted in leaving the church and the suburb where we were living to relocate almost 700 kilometres south. My wife managed to obtain a transfer in her job about eight months later.

> **We can still be in the center of God's will for our lives, even when our world is suddenly turned upside down.**

This may simply mean God has a new chapter planned for our lives—a new season or new adventure in Him.

I have known Christian people who try to do everything they can to keep the same easy, comfortable life to which they are accustomed. Some of these people knew God was shaking things up in their lives, but they were comfortable where they were and really did not want to move or change anything that might threaten their existing comfortable lives.

Elijah's Victory, Part 1

We can stand and rejoice in the hope we have in God's Word, especially when problems, trials, or troubles come, or when things do not go to plan.

> Therefore, since we have been made right in God's sight by faith, we have peace[15] with God because of what Jesus Christ our Lord has done for us. Because of our faith, Christ has brought us into this place of undeserved privilege where we now stand, and we confidently and joyfully look forward to sharing God's glory. We can rejoice, too, when we run into problems and trials, for we know that they help us develop endurance. And endurance develops strength of character, and character strengthens our confident hope of salvation. And this hope will not lead to disappointment. For we know how dearly God loves us, because he has given us the Holy Spirit to fill our hearts with his love. (Romans 5:1–5, NLT)

When problems or trials come into our lives, they produce endurance (perseverance, NKJV) in us, endurance produces strength of Christian character, and Christian character strengthens our confident hope of salvation. We cannot have true Christian character or hope without problems, trials, or troubles in our lives.

If we have this hope in our God, His love can be poured into our hearts, and from there into our family, world, and church by the Holy Spirit, who was given to us on the day of Pentecost. Let us all take His love into our dying world every day.

---

15. Some manuscripts read let us have peace (footnote in the NLT Bible).

When Life Becomes Uncomfortable

I love gardening. Some types of orchids that I grew in my greenhouse only produced beautiful flowers after they were stressed, either by cold weather or a lack of rain or watering. Without this stress, these orchids never flowered.

As Christian people, we cannot produce the life and fruit God requires without stress caused by wilderness experiences or changes in our lives.

The twelve disciples were in a boat toward the middle of the sea of Galilee, at night-time, battling a ferocious storm (Matthew 14:22–33). Shortly before dawn, Jesus appeared to them, walking on the water in the storm. He said one word, "Come" (verse 29).

Peter stepped out of the boat because he believed the word of Jesus. His faith in Jesus's word was enough to overcome the storm, his circumstances, his fear of drowning, as well as the unkind, unsupportive, and criticizing words directed at him by the other disciples in the boat.

The temptation when things start to go wrong is to start praying and rebuking the devil and every evil spirit we can think of.

However, we must realise God may be leading us into difficult or uncomfortable situations so that He can teach us new spiritual lessons. If we choose to stay in our comfort zone, we will miss these lessons and preparation for a new spiritual level in God.

When I was seven or eight years old, my older sister and I were asked to play our musical instruments on a stage in front of a small crowd. When our turn came, my fingers froze on my instrument as I looked at the people watching us. I could not play my instrument because of my stage fright, so I was crying as I ran off the stage. I never wanted to speak or play in front of a crowd ever again. God has been patient with me over many years as He has enabled me to overcome my fear of public speaking.

I was attending a large Pentecostal church in the city of Brisbane. Many of the youth group, including me, were part of an evangelistic activity one Saturday night in the middle of the city. I was part of the team who were to talk to people about accepting Jesus Christ as their personal Saviour as we mingled among the crowd that gathered.

This was very confronting and uncomfortable for me, as I had never shared my faith with a stranger before. I always felt inferior to others and was unsure of what to say or how to say it. I began talking to one young man. To my surprise, he knelt in front of me on the hard concrete to give his life to Jesus.

God had taken me out of my comfort zone.

We need to be prepared to leave our comfortable life and follow where God leads us, despite everything that is happening, our fears of what may happen, or what others may say, think, or tell us to do.

> **If you or I do not get out of our comfortable Christian existence, we will not fulfill God's plan for our lives.**

If we choose to stay in our comfort zone, we may become like the Dead Sea–dead to spiritual life because water flows into the sea, but it has no outlet. The salt levels build up so that there is no or little life that can survive there.

Personal Application

- How does your faith in the words of Jesus compare to Peter's in Matthew chapter 14?

- Are you willing to step out of the boat at the command of Jesus?

- How do you know if your circumstances are caused by the evil one or if God is leading you in a new direction?

- Are you comfortable in your Christian life or ministry? If you are, are you willing to allow God to change things to make you uncomfortable?

- Are you willing to follow God, even when your comfortable life is turned upside down?

- Have you been, or are you now, in a situation where circumstances are difficult or wrong, where you feel God is far away, or you are in a spiritual wilderness? What do you need to do to trust God is leading you in this?

LESSON 6

God's Plan Before Our Life Changes

Then the word of the LORD came to him, saying, "Arise, go to Zarephath, which belongs to Sidon, and dwell there. See, I have commanded a widow there to provide for you." (1 Kings 17:8, 9)

God had a plan for Elijah before the brook dried up. When the brook dried up it did not catch God by surprise. God never had to say, "Oh dear, I never saw that coming. I will have to command some angels to drop water in the brook so Elijah can stay there."

No!

> **God had already chosen a widow to take care of Elijah, while he was watching the brook dry up.**

My first secular work after graduating from university was based in a small sugar town in North Queensland. I had to travel 1,270 kilometres from the state capital, Brisbane, where I was living at Mum and Dad's place. This required a two-day drive in my small car to arrive at an unfamiliar destination where I did not know anyone. Everything I owned was packed into that car.

I arrived in that town late in the afternoon and checked into a motel. After I was settled in, I attended a church meeting that night at a local Pentecostal church. At that meeting I discovered there were two young guys of similar age to me who were moving into a three-bedroom house the very next day. They were looking for another young guy to move into that house to help share the costs.

God had a plan for me before I arrived in that town. He provided a bedroom and everything I needed to live for the next two years, including bathroom, stove, cooking facilities, and furniture.

I experienced a similar provision of God when I had to travel to my last full-time, secular job. One week before I was due to arrive at my new destination to commence work, I received an email with the details of someone who had a four-bedroom house with a bedroom I could rent. That house had everything I needed to live for the next eight months, including all the material things I needed that I could not pack in my car. God provided again before I arrived in that town.

The disciples of Jesus, like so many Christian people today, had the belief that anything that goes wrong in life is the result of sin, including sickness.

In John chapter 9, the disciples asked Jesus whose fault it was that a man was blind from birth.

God's Plan Before Our Life Changes

"Now as Jesus passed by, He saw a man who was blind from birth. And His disciples asked Him, saying, 'Rabbi, who sinned, this man or his parents, that he was born blind?'" (John 9:1, 2).

Jesus replied, "Neither this man nor his parents sinned, but that *the works of God should be revealed in him*" (John 9:3, emphasis added).

Jesus told his disciples that the purpose of the man's blindness was to reveal God's glory when He healed him, as recorded in verses 6 and 7.

God had a plan to heal this man's blindness before he was born.

Jesus's words are so true in our daily lives. "Therefore do not be like them. For your Father knows the things you have need of before you ask Him" (Matthew 6:8).

Further on in this chapter, part of the Sermon on the Mount, Jesus teaches that God provides all our daily needs, including food, clothes, and shelter. We are not to worry about these things:

> Therefore do not worry, saying, "What shall we eat?" or "What shall we drink?" or "What shall we wear?" For after all these things the Gentiles seek. For your heavenly Father knows that you need all these things. But seek first the kingdom of God and His righteousness, and all these things shall be added to you. Therefore do not worry about tomorrow, for tomorrow will worry about its own things. Sufficient for the day is its own trouble. (Matthew 6:31–34)

If I genuinely trust that God knows what He is doing, life is so much easier. I am free from worrying about the future, worrying about tomorrow. My God has a plan. I do not know what may happen tomorrow, but I can trust Him with my every tomorrow.

> **My circumstances do not dictate or control the future, because my God does.**

When my wife and I were the church pastors in North Queensland, we visited a pastor and his wife from a church in another small town, and whom we had known for many years. Before we left, God had told us to give him twenty dollars while we were still there. We shared with him how God had told us to give him the money, which we did.

To our surprise, tears flowed from his eyes. He told us his wife had found some nice business shirts for him that cost ten dollars each on special from a local shop. They couldn't afford this until some support money came the following week. They were so excited about God's provision, because now they could buy two shirts when he and his wife had been believing God for the money to buy one.

The apostle Paul knew the secret to being content in every situation he faced in his life. That secret was knowing God gave him strength to overcome his circumstances, no matter how unfair they seemed to him.

> Do not be anxious about anything, but in every situation, by prayer and petition, with thanksgiving, present your requests to God.…I am not saying this because I am in need, for I have learned to be content whatever the circumstances. I know what

it is to be in need, and I know what it is to have plenty. I have learned the secret of being content in any and every situation, whether well fed or hungry, whether living in plenty or in want. I can do all this through him who gives me strength. (Philippians 4:6, 11–13, NIV)

This enabled Paul to ask for the following prayer in Ephesians 6:19, 20 (NIV): "Pray also for me, that whenever I speak, words may be given me so that I will fearlessly make known the mystery of the gospel, for which I am an ambassador in chains. Pray that I may declare it fearlessly, as I should."

Paul was a prisoner in chains, through no fault of his own. Acts chapter 21 reveals how he was arrested. The charges against him were false. He was completely innocent, yet he spent the rest of his life in prison and/or chains.

He did not write to everyone he could about how unjust it was that he was in this horrible prison. Paul never asked anyone to pray for his deliverance from this painful experience, or to publicise any sort of campaign to get him out of jail or chains. He never complained about how difficult his situation was. There was no bitterness or anger concerning his situation, nor did he ask anyone to pray against his circumstances.

Instead, he asked people to pray that he would fearlessly make known the gospel to anyone who would listen, the good news that Jesus Christ died to set people free. Paul asked that with God's grace he would be bold in declaring this good news. That is the most important thing of all.

How different was Paul's attitude toward the difficulties in his life when compared with the attitude many Christians demonstrate in today's world?

Elijah's Victory, Part 1

Too many Christians want someone to pray against their circumstances or the people who oppose, criticise, or ostracise them instead of having a similar attitude to that of Paul. They want God to instantly deliver them from any situation or circumstance that is not comfortable or a blessing, or from anything they don't like.

God had a plan for Paul's life before his world was turned upside down. That plan was revealed to Paul when the Lord talked to him one night, after he had appeared before the Jewish leadership, the Sanhedrin, at the request of the Roman commander at Jerusalem (Acts 22:22—23:10): "But the following night the Lord stood by him and said,[16] 'Be of good cheer, Paul; for as you have testified for Me in Jerusalem, so you must also bear witness at Rome'" (Acts 23:11).

God has a plan for you and me and our families. His plan does not change because of our circumstances, health, or finances. We need to see that our source of supply is not the income from our job, business, investments, or pension. These are simply the means God chooses to supply our needs. If God chooses to change His method of providing for us that does not in any way affect His ability to do so.

There was a time when my wife and I were short on money. Our financial situation was almost desperate, juggling paying everyday bills and monthly house payments. We were behind in our house mortgage payments, and it seemed to me that if God did not intervene, we were in danger of losing our house.

So, we prayed and trusted God.

---

16. Take courage (footnote in the NKJV Bible).

God's Plan Before Our Life Changes

We did not ask our church people for money, put out a prayer request, or let anyone know of our financial situation except God. He provided, as He always does, as a father provides for his children.

My dad sent us some money in the mail, even though he did not know our situation, and that was the only time he ever did. I did not tell him about our circumstances, but God had our circumstances in His hand. Dad's letter contained a cheque that was dated before we had prayed about our financial situation. God's provision was on the way before we needed it.

Do we really believe and trust God still has a plan for us in the middle of the week, or when things are not working out the way we think they should?

Personal Application

- Do other people notice you trust in God to provide your daily needs, or do you rely on your income, from whatever source, for your provision?

- Do you really trust that God has everything in control, that He has a plan before your circumstances change?

- If you do, how does this belief affect your daily attitude toward:

    » Difficulties or trials that come in your life?

    » People who criticize you or tell you that your situation is impossible, especially if they are close Christian friends?

    » Finances, especially when you are struggling or finances seem so limited?

- Is your attitude toward material possessions different from that of others who do not know your God as you do?

- Is there any attitude toward people or circumstances you need to change?

LESSON 7

God Provides in Unexpected Ways

Then the word of the LORD came to him, saying, "Arise, go to Zarephath, which belongs to Sidon, and dwell there. See, I have commanded a widow there to provide for you." So he arose and went to Zarephath. And when he came to the gate of the city, indeed a widow was there gathering sticks.... "I do not have bread, only a handful of flour in a bin, and a little oil in a jar[17]; and see, I am gathering a couple of sticks that I may go in and prepare it for myself and my son, that we may eat it, and die."
(1 Kings 17:8–10, 12)

The widow God had prepared to look after Elijah was poor, with no food left (verses 10 and 12 of 1 Kings 17), because picking up sticks was a servant's job. If she was rich enough to have a servant, the servant would

---

17. Lit. pitcher or water jar (footnote in the NKJV Bible).

have been picking up sticks.[18]

Elijah could have looked at the widow, saw she was in trouble feeding herself and her son, and then questioned God's leading. "How can this poor woman, who is about to die of starvation, look after me? God, what are you doing?"

He may have been tempted to think that this lady was not the right widow God had selected to look after him during the drought. Elijah may have thought, "It was nice while I was at the brook. That was my hard time, my desert experience, which was a bit lonely. I had to endure those long nights alone by the brook. Some of those were a bit chilly. Therefore, I think I deserve a nice, rich widow to look after me, who owns a warm house, which has a comfortable room for me, with lots of nice, choice food to eat."

However, that was not God's plan. God was teaching Elijah to trust that He had everything under control.

> **Elijah had to learn to trust God, no matter how unexpected God's leading seemed to his natural mind.**

I have found in my life that God specialises in providing for me in unexpected ways.

In my agricultural consulting business there was a dispute regarding some work I completed for one of my clients. Legal action was threatened against me. It was suggested by others experienced with this type of dispute

---

18. *Matthew Henry's Commentary.*

that I organise a senior consultant to travel to the area and act as mediator. This all had to be at my expense.

The mediator recommended I repay my consulting fees to this client to avoid litigation, which I did to the satisfaction of both the client and myself. The cost of resolving this dispute stretched my finances almost to breaking point at that time.

After this stressful situation was resolved, the mediator asked me to accept work for him in the local area. I agreed to this on a part-time basis. The payments I received for this extra work, which continued for a few years, were much more than my cost to resolve the situation. If I never had the dispute with the original client, I would never have received that extra income. God provided for my finances through such a difficult circumstance in a way I never could have expected.

I believe it was difficult for Elijah to head for Zarephath in obedience to God's voice. Zarephath was Jezebel's hometown and the world headquarters of Baal worship. She had installed the 400 Baal prophets in the land of Israel.

Ahab and Jezebel were still looking for Elijah in order to kill him because they blamed him for the drought. He could have said (or thought), "God, what if her relatives who live in Zarephath recognise me? If they alert Jezebel that I have come to town, how are you going to protect me then?"

God, however, was still leading him even if his circumstances were difficult or changing.

One weekend, when we were the pastor and wife at a previous church, I had been sick for a few days. Sunday morning I was no different. I was a Spirit-filled pastor who believed in praying for God to heal people, but I was not well at all. I could not physically stand to preach.

When the time came for preaching in the service, I told the people I was sick and could not physically preach. Then I said, "If anyone has anything to share, please do so," and sat down in the front row. Three people from the congregation who were there that morning shared for about five to ten minutes each. What they said flowed together so well it was fantastic. I grew in God, those three grew in God, all the congregation attending that day did as well, and I could not have organised the service better if I had preached that morning.

I learnt again it was not about me, but about what God can do. (Of course, anyone in a senior leadership position of a church must know the people they allow to preach or share, for obvious reasons.)

When King David, with 600 of his men, returned to Ziklag after being expelled from the Philistine army, they were confronted with a burnt city. Amalekites had stolen their material possessions and taken their families captive (1 Samuel 30:1–4).

God had an unusual way of leading them to reclaim what was stolen. An Egyptian slave who was almost dead from lack of food and water directed King David and his men to the Amalekites' camp where they were able to recover all their families and possessions (1 Samuel 30:11–20).

Too often we as Christians miss God's leading or provision because we have already ruled out that person or that circumstance. Sometimes we think we are above or beyond learning from that person or circumstance because we are now so spiritual. We have grown in our spiritual life and cannot go back there.

The Pharisees sent temple guards to arrest Jesus (John 7:32); but they did not arrest Him.

> Finally the temple guards went back to the chief priests and the Pharisees, who asked them, "Why didn't you bring him in?"
>
> "No one ever spoke the way this man does," the guards replied.
>
> "You mean he has deceived you also?" the Pharisees retorted. "Have any of the rulers or of the Pharisees believed in him? No! But this mob that knows nothing of the law—there is a curse on them."
> (John 7:45–49, NIV)

When Nicodemus questioned why the other Pharisees had already judged Jesus without hearing him (verses 50, 51) they answered him, "Are you from Galilee, too? Look into it, and you will find that a prophet does not come out of Galilee." (verse 52, NIV).

The story of Jesus miraculously healing a man who had been blind from birth (John chapter 9) was discussed earlier (within lesson 6). The crowd brought him to the Pharisees (verse 13), who investigated his healing because it occurred on the Sabbath (verses 14–33).

During this investigation, the Pharisees were divided about who Jesus was because he healed the blind man on the Sabbath. "Some of the Pharisees said, 'This man is not from God, for he does not[19] keep the Sabbath.' Others said, 'How can a man who is a sinner do such signs?' And there was a division among them" (verse 16).

After their investigation, they excommunicated from the temple the blind man who Jesus had healed, because he dared to declare that Jesus was sent from God.

---

19. Observe (footnote in the NKJV Bible).

Elijah's Victory, Part 1

"They answered and said to him, 'You were completely born in sins, and are you teaching us?' And they[20] cast him out" (John 9:34).

The Pharisees could not be taught about the things of God from anyone whom they thought was beneath them spiritually. They also rejected Jesus as the Messiah because he did not fulfil their religious laws.

When I began work in my professional career, I was only the junior in the team. A more senior person was coming to talk to each of us in the office where I worked. This person was one of the top leaders of the profession, well-known and respected in our state, nation, and in some overseas countries. I felt God say to me, "Tell him that whatever his circumstances, your God will meet his needs."

I said to God, "How can I, as a junior only recently started, say this to such a world-class professional?"

After hesitating for a few moments, I said to God on the Friday that I would say these words when I talked to him on the following Monday when he was scheduled to meet with me.

On Sunday afternoon, I received a telephone call with the sad news that this highly rated professional man had passed away. I had missed my God-given opportunity to share God's Word with this man, because I felt inferior. I looked at my circumstances compared to his.

May each one who claims to know God never feel inferior compared to others who need God's Word, even if this costs us our reputation, friends, income, or threatens our very lives.

I pray that we learn that God can use anybody or any circumstance in our lives to teach us more of His ways. We

---

20. Excommunicated him (footnote in the NKJV Bible).

must simply trust and obey, regardless of how or by whom God chooses to lead us.

True faith is taking risks by simply trusting and obeying despite God's ways being unexpected. That is what the widow did in verses 10 and 15 of 1 Kings 17 when she obeyed the words of Elijah.

> **Faith is not believing when we see or know what God is going to do. It is obeying what God says to do, even when we do not know what the result may be.**

Joshua told the priests in Joshua chapter 3 to carry the ark to the edge of the Jordan River. When their feet touched the water, God would stop its flow so that the people could cross over on dry ground.

What physical evidence did the priests have that if they obeyed Joshua's word they would not drown in the powerful current of the Jordan River in full flood?

None at all.

They just had the word of Joshua. They hoped and prayed that he had heard God correctly. The miracle occurred when they acted on Joshua's words—the floodwater stopped flowing.

What physical evidence did Shadrach, Meshach, and Abednego have that they would not be burned alive in the fiery furnace when they refused to bow to a very large gold statue set up by King Nebuchadnezzar (Daniel chapter 3)?

None at all.

God kept them safe in the blazing furnace because they refused to worship the statue, or false god.

What physical evidence did Daniel have that God would keep him safe when he was thrown into a den of hungry lions (Daniel chapter 6)?

None at all.

He continued praying to God despite the threat of the lion's den. God delivered him because he obeyed God rather than the king's law.

What physical evidence do we have that if we obey the still, small voice of God it will not flop, fail, or cause us embarrassment and pain?

None at all.

God simply wants us to obey without knowing if it will work out or not, without knowing the end result.

Some people must rigorously check out the person and any so-called word from the Lord before they obey it. It is almost like needing a character reference for a job interview.

How many words have you given in the name of the Lord? How many have come to pass? Give me the names of three people who can testify that you gave them a word that came to pass. When I have all that information, and I have checked out your reputation from the church you attend, then I might obey what you said was a word from the Lord. Cannot be too careful you know; I never want the devil to mislead me.

Sometimes we miss God's leading by waiting for confirmation we cannot ignore. Some Christians who demand such confirmation from God or others do so not as a way to be sure of God's leading but as an excuse for inaction.

Faith is more than words; it involves our actions. In Jesus's own words, "if you love me, keep my commandments" (John 14:15).

Do you believe in God? Then your actions should match your faith.

God Provides in Unexpected Ways

You and I need to obey what God says even if His leading takes us in unexpected directions. We must be obedient without trying to figure it all out in our human minds, without any guarantee other than God's Word that it will happen. The life of Wilma Rudolph is an example of someone who never gave up on God's leading despite her circumstances.

Wilma Rudolph[21] is known as the polio victim who won three Olympic gold medals. Polio took a toll on Wilma as a child. For six years she wore braces and could not walk, but she believed the braces would someday come off. The doctor was doubtful Wilma would ever walk correctly, but he encouraged her to exercise.

Wilma did not understand that she might be permanently handicapped. She thought that if a little exercise was good, a lot must be very good. When her parents were away, Wilma would take off the braces and try again and again to walk unaided.

When she was eleven, she told her doctor, "I have something to show you." Wilma removed her braces and walked across the room. She never put them on again.

Wilma wanted to play sports. After some false starts at basketball, she finally confronted her coach, saying, "If you give me ten minutes a day, I will give you in return a world-class athlete." The coach laughed uncontrollably but agreed to give Wilma the time.

When basketball season was over, Wilma turned to track. By age fourteen she was on the track team, and by sixteen she was encouraged to prepare for the Olympics.

Wilma Rudolph won a bronze medal at the 1956 Olympics and three gold medals at the 1960 games.

---

21. Her story is extracted from Norwood (2017).

Personal Application

- Has the small voice of God told you to go into difficult situations or talk to difficult people?
- Have you obeyed God?
- Are you trusting and obeying God's small voice even if you do not understand where or why He is leading you?
- Is there anything you need to do or change after answering the questions above?
- Read the story of Wilma Rudolph again.
- What can the Lord achieve through you if you keep on trying despite your failures or limitations?
- **Remember:** God does not care how many times you fail trying to do what He leads you to do. However, He does care if you give up or refuse to try again.

LESSON 8

God Helps Those With Weak Faith

And he called to her and said, "Please bring me a little water in a cup, that I may drink." And as she was going to get it, he called to her and said, "Please bring me a morsel of bread in your hand." So she said, "As the LORD your God lives, I do not have bread, only a handful of flour in a bin, and a little oil in a jar[22]; and see, I am gathering a couple of sticks that I may go in and prepare it for myself and my son, that we may eat it, and die." (1 Kings 17:10–12)

We can read this Bible story and easily miss an important lesson God wants to teach us.

This story reveals more than God miraculously suppling Elijah's daily food and water during the drought. There is another person in the story—the widow of Zarephath, who

---

22. Lit. pitcher or water jar (footnote in the NKJV Bible).

was close to dying of starvation. A widow who had weak faith in Elijah's God.

God cared for the widow because He was still in control despite her desperate situation. She was a non-Jew, a gentile, who was not part of God's chosen people. A person whom many of the religious people of Elijah's time despised as worthless or unimportant to God's purposes on the earth.

There is no favouritism with God (Romans 3:21–24; Galatians 2:6). He cares for anyone who comes to Him by faith in Jesus Christ's death and resurrection, regardless of race or skin colour. God's plan was to strengthen the widow's faith and save her and her son from dying. He was going to use Elijah to do it.

> **God's purpose was to teach Elijah that someone else's needs should be the central focus of his life, rather than his personal circumstances.**

We must also learn the lesson that God's number one priority for us is not necessarily our comfortable life in terms of material possessions or resources to live our daily lives. As we live on this planet, our first priority should be to challenge people to know who our God really is. Our second priority should be to encourage people to grow in their faith in the living God of the universe, our Lord and Saviour Jesus Christ.

God had chosen this poor widow to look after Elijah's needs to survive the drought.

God Helps Those With Weak Faith

Elijah, a total stranger to this widow, asked her for a drink. She did not hesitate to get it. This showed she was willing to share with a stranger the very thing that was so scarce at that time—water.

As she was getting water, Elijah asked for bread. Notice the widow's response in 1 Kings 17:12. She replied to Elijah's request for bread with the phrase, "As the LORD your God lives." How did she know Elijah was a servant of God? She had never met him before that moment.

She lived in Zarephath where worship of Baal was the dominant religion. She did not say "as Baal lives" but "as the LORD your God lives." How did she obtain faith in the God of Elijah? I do not know; the Bible does not tell us. Even though she had that faith, she was getting ready to have one last meal before both she and her son were going to die of starvation. She recognised who God was, but her limited or weak faith did not believe He loved or cared for her enough to change her life-threatening situation.

John the Baptist, on the other hand, declared to everyone who would listen exactly who God was:

> The next day John saw Jesus coming toward him and said, "Look, the Lamb of God, who takes away the sin of the world! This is the one I meant when I said, 'A man who comes after me has surpassed me because he was before me.' I myself did not know him, but the reason I came baptizing with water was that he might be revealed to Israel." (John 1:29–31, NIV)

He also announced that Jesus was the Son of God (John 1:34).

"But when John rebuked Herod the tetrarch because of his marriage to Herodias, his brother's wife, and all the other evil things he had done, Herod added this to them all: He locked John up in prison." (Luke 3:19, 20, NIV).

John the Baptist sent two of his disciples to ask Jesus if He really was the one he had earlier publicly proclaimed (Matthew 11:2, 3).

"Jesus replied, 'Go back and report to John what you hear and see: The blind receive sight, the lame walk, those who have leprosy[23] are cleansed, the deaf hear, the dead are raised, and the good news is proclaimed to the poor. Blessed is anyone who does not stumble on account of me.'" (Matthew 11:4–6, NIV).

John the Baptist doubted what he had so confidently and publicly professed because he was now in prison. He allowed his circumstances to weaken his faith in God.

Jesus Christ did not send John the Baptist's disciples back with a rebuke to John for allowing his circumstances to undermine his faith. God always encourages us to grow in our faith in Him despite our circumstances.

Jesus's response to John's two disciples in Matthew 11:4–6 quoted Isaiah 35:5 and 6. Isaiah's prophecy includes these words immediately before the words Jesus quoted: "Strengthen the feeble hands, steady the knees that give way; say to those with fearful hearts, 'Be strong, do not fear; your God will come, he will come with vengeance with divine retribution he will come to save you'" (Isaiah 35:3, 4, NIV).

When Jesus healed large crowds of people, he warned them not to make him known (Matthew 12:15–21). This fulfils the prophecy of the servant of the Lord found in Isaiah 42:1–4, according to Matthew.

---

23. The Greek word traditionally translated leprosy was used for various diseases affecting the skin (footnote in the NIV Bible).

God Helps Those With Weak Faith

Verse 3 of Isaiah's prophecy says, "A bruised reed He will not break, and a smouldering wick He will not snuff out. In faithfulness he will bring forth justice" (NIV). Both a bruised reed and smouldering (or dimly burning) wick are very delicate, easily broken, or extinguished.

God never rebukes us when our faith is delicate (or weak) or easily destroyed. This description fits the widow of Zarephath, John the Baptist, and many Christian people today. No matter how weak our faith, or how desperate our situation, God wants to strengthen our faith in Him and supply the answer(s) we are looking for.

The widow confessed God as the *living* God. He was *your* God (not *my* God).

There are many people today who recognise God, or say they believe in God. They may go to church, sing songs, and say all the right Christian things at the right time. When the circumstances of their life get tough, they give up on God, the Bible, church, and sadly sometimes even life itself.

They give up because they may *know of God*, but they do not *know God* personally. Their faith believes that although God can care for someone else, He does not care for them personally. Once anyone does know God personally, life can never be the same, despite their circumstances.

In our society we can all too often descend, I use this word deliberately, into thinking we are no more than a computer number or a statistic. That is one of the biggest lies of the devil today.

God loves everyone. We matter to Him today and every day we wake up breathing. God cares for every one of our situations or circumstances, including our problems, families, sicknesses, or diseases, even if our faith is only weak or not where it should be.

Elijah's Victory, Part 1

Jesus cared for a guy possessed with so many demons that no one could tame him. This man wandered in the cemetery, naked and bleeding from where he was continually cutting himself with stones, trying to stop the terrible voices in his head (Mark 5:1–20). Jesus and His disciples crossed the lake in a boat to deliver such a man. He is the same God today that can deliver you and me from every lie of the devil.

Many Christian people think that the image of God in them is tarnished or made dull because of their sinful nature. However, the image is still there, even if we cannot see it. We may need to clean or polish it to make it shine better, but it is still there!

> **You and I matter to God. He wants to increase our level of faith in Him.**

God wants to encourage us so that He can use our life as an example of someone who has been changed by His power. Let us allow him to do what He wants to do in our lives today.

Most of us, if we are honest, have times in our lives when we think or believe (thanks to the devil's lies) that circumstances in our lives are so hard that to continue in our Christian life is just not worth it. We may feel or believe that our lives are almost meaningless, or we are just existing from day to day. It may appear to us what we are doing in our lives just does not mean what it used to in our eyes, or does not factor into God's purposes or plan for our lives.

Once when I was working in my secular job, I started to question why I was working in that job. Nobody I had talked to about God seemed remotely interested or challenged by the power of God. My life at that time did not seem to have any spiritual meaning at all. So, I talked to God about it (actually, more like I complained that God was not doing enough through my testimony).

My work involved driving long distances to many locations throughout the state of Queensland. This meant staying overnight for a few days or a week, or occasionally longer, each time. God said to me, "Make a list of the names of those who have shared motel or hotel rooms or apartments with you over the years through your work."

When I did, I soon realised that list included everyone in my specialised type of work. At some time or other I had shared a room, apartment, adjoining rooms, or a campsite in the bush with all those people. Everybody knew what I believed from observing my life at work and socially afterward.

Only a few weeks after I wrote this list, one of the guys said to me in the 4WD truck as we were driving out bush, "Jim we all know what you stand for and believe. We respect that, it's just some of us may agree with you, and some may not."

All I did was sow some seeds. God will do the rest in His time and in His way. I was reminded of Paul's words in 1 Corinthians 3:5-8.

> Who then is Paul, and who is Apollos, but ministers through whom you believed, as the Lord gave to each one? I planted, Apollos watered, but God gave the increase. So then neither he who plants is anything, nor he who waters, but God who gives the increase. Now he who plants and he who waters are one, and each one will receive his own reward according to his own labor.

I believe sowing seeds of God's goodness and grace to all we meet should be our motivation or reason for everything we do in our daily lives.

Some people tell me "I am not too bad under the circumstances (or considering the circumstances)." It is time to get out from under the circumstances to see the circumstances change by the power of our God. If our God is really on the throne, then nothing that happens to you or me or our circumstances can ever change that. Nothing.

In Acts 1:4 and 5, Jesus promised the disciples they would be baptised in the Holy Spirit; something supernatural and exciting. The disciples' response was to ask if He was going to restore the kingdom to Israel (verse 6). They were more concerned about the restoration of the kingdom of the Jews and overthrowing the dreaded Romans at the time than about something supernatural that was about to happen. Their situation and needs become their focus instead of what Jesus was teaching them.

In my words they were really saying, "That's nice, Jesus, that something is about to happen, but how is this going to affect us? How will this solve our immediate problems? We need You to deal with the oppression of our people under the dreaded Roman authorities."

God wants us to focus on His purposes in our everyday lives instead of our needs or difficult circumstances: "But seek first the kingdom of God and His righteousness, and all these things shall be added to you" (Matthew 6:33).

Too often, when we as Christians ask God to help us in our time of need or our challenging circumstances, our prayers are all about *our* feelings, *our* circumstances, *our* problems, *us* and *our* little cocoon in the world.

God Helps Those With Weak Faith

I believe God wants to minister His love for other people through us, not hear us complaining about all that is happening to us, how our life is just not fair, or how our situation or circumstances are all His fault. He leads us to lonely, poor, despised people who nobody cares for except God. All too often we miss it because we are preoccupied with us being the center of our universe.

Paul and Silas were beaten with rods by the authorities in Philippi and then jailed because Paul had cast out an evil spirit from a slave girl (Acts 16:16–24). Instead of complaining to God about their horrible situation, they prayed and sang hymns to God at midnight while the other prisoners were listening to them (verse 25). They were not praying or singing quietly under their breath, as they wanted everybody who was listening to hear of God's love and faithfulness despite their unfair circumstances.

God sent an earthquake to open all the prison doors and cause all the chains to fall off the prisoners. As a result, the Philippian jailer and his household believed in God and were baptised. The jailer washed their wounds and prepared food for them (verses 26–34).

I believe if you and I pray and sing to God despite our circumstances, we will see God perform miracles and others will come to know our God just as the jailer did in this story.

Steven Hill was the evangelist associated with a revival at Brownsville Assembly of God, Pensacola, Florida, USA. He wrote a book titled *The Pursuit of Revival*. In his book Steve challenges us to examine what really motivates us. When God moves in meetings, nothing of our circumstances or needs seems to matter anymore compared to witnessing God visibly change someone else's life.

Anyone who asks God for a miracle or to help them must first believe that He exists and have faith, no matter how small or weak, that this God can change their circumstances (Hebrews 11:6).

I have had many people tell me that they do not believe in this God or religious nonsense. Some have also claimed that science has proved the Bible is wrong and that God does not exist.

However, some of these same people ring or text asking my wife or I to pray when they are in a terrible situation or something bad happens to a close friend or someone in their family. I often want to say to them (but would never do), "How can you ask me to pray to a God that you told me does not exist or you do not believe in?"

This widow already had faith in God before Elijah showed up. Now she was asked to put her weak faith into action despite her circumstances. She had to trust God that if she fed Elijah first, there would be enough remaining to feed herself and her son. Physically it was impossible.

> And Elijah said to her, "Do not fear; go and do as you have said, but make me a small cake from it first, and bring it to me; and afterward make some for yourself and your son. For thus says the LORD God of Israel: 'The bin of flour shall not be used up, nor shall the jar of oil run dry, until the day the LORD sends rain on the earth.'"
>
> So she went away and did according to the word of Elijah; and she and he and her household ate for many days. The bin of flour was not used up, nor did the jar of oil run dry, according to the word of the LORD which He spoke by Elijah. (1 Kings 17:13–16)

God Helps Those With Weak Faith

She obeyed what Elijah told her was the word of the LORD God of Israel, and God performed the miracle. Elijah, the widow, and her son enjoyed the provision of bread every day until the LORD sent rain upon the earth.

If you or I were in a similar situation, would we obey the words of the prophet?

Elijah was learning this event was more than God leading him to someone who could supply food and shelter for him; it was about understanding that God was concerned for this poor widow (who had weak faith) and her son, both of whom had been overlooked by the world. They were confronting the end of their lives. If God had not intervened, they would not have survived the famine caused by the drought.

He cares enough about you and your situation to accomplish a miracle for you too. God loves the worst of sinners. He loves the lonely person who thinks God has abandoned them.

God cares for everyone on the planet. He wants all of us to see who He really is so we can experience His love for ourselves. Once anyone sees who our God really is, they are never the same again. That is why Elijah was able to pray what he did to bring down God's fire in 1 Kings 18:36, 37:

> And it came to pass, at the time of the offering of the evening sacrifice, that Elijah the prophet came near and said, "LORD God of Abraham, Isaac, and Israel, let it be known this day that You are God in Israel and I am Your servant, and that I have done all these things at Your word. Hear me, O LORD, hear me, that this people may know that You are the LORD God, and that You have turned their hearts back to You again."

Elijah now understood that God's purpose in all that he learnt was to bring the nation face to face with who God really was, not so he could be remembered as the prophet who brought down fire from heaven.

There was nothing in Elijah's prayer about God proving that he, Elijah, was right, and that the false prophets were wrong. His prayer was that God would turn the hearts of the people back to Him by bringing them face to face with who He really was.

How would you or I pray in Elijah's situation?

Personal Application

- Do YOU believe God can change YOUR circumstances today, or do you think He is more concerned with someone else who you think is more important in God's kingdom than you?
- Can you see or focus on the needs of someone else, even when you are in a difficult situation, or your needs are not being met?
- Is your prayer life mainly about you and your needs, or can you pray for others despite your circumstances?
- Is your faith in God weak, so that you are ready to give up on God or life itself?
- What can you learn from this lesson that you can apply to your life today?
- What can you learn from this lesson to minister to someone who is ready to give up on God, church, or life itself?

LESSON 9

God Provides Our Daily Bread

So she went away and did according to the word of Elijah; and she and he and her household ate for many days. The bin of flour was not used up, nor did the jar of oil run dry, according to the word of the LORD which He spoke by Elijah. (1 Kings 17:15, 16)

God provided for the widow, her son, and Elijah every day by supernaturally extending the small amount of oil and meal (flour). When they checked the cupboard every morning, there it was again, the same amount they had had prior to preparing yesterday's food. This was just enough for what they needed that day. Most commentators believe this continued for over or close to two years.

This provision reminds me of part of the Lord's Prayer in Matthew chapter 6 (part of the Sermon on the Mount) and in Luke chapter 11, "Give us this day, our daily bread."

> **God has promised our daily bread, or what we need each day to live in our society.**

Notice Jesus did not say "God will provide what you need now for next week, next month, or next year." There is nothing wrong with budgeting our finances for what we may need at a future date. If we trust God day by day, it keeps us humble and in right relationship with Him, regardless of what the future may hold. This allows us to overcome worrying about how we can pay for what we need tomorrow.

In Matthew 6:34, Jesus tells us, "Therefore do not worry about tomorrow, for tomorrow will worry about its own things. Sufficient for the day is its own trouble."

Time and time again, when major bills like council rates, car registration, electricity, or house insurance come, I do not have the money to pay the bill. Yet God always makes sure I have enough to pay this when it is due, or a few days before for internet banking purposes.

While my wife and I were the ministers in a church in North Queensland, we received a letter with money in it. We did not recognise the handwriting. There was no return or sender's address on the back, nor had we asked our church people for money. God provided for our daily needs through this gift, even though we had no idea where or who it came from.

The Egyptians had grain to eat despite a severe famine caused by drought because the people obeyed Joseph, who delivered a God-given interpretation of Pharaoh's dreams (Genesis chapter 41).

A recently widowed lady with a desperate financial need came to the prophet Elisha (2 Kings 4:1–6). She obeyed

Elisha's word. God miraculously provided the finances needed to pay her creditors, with enough left to provide for her and her two sons. God always provides for us in His way and in His time when we are faithful to obey His voice and follow Him.

Jesus miraculously fed 5,000 men (plus women and children) from five barley loaves and two small fish (Mathew 14:13-21; Luke 9:10-17; John 6:1-14). He also fed 4,000 men (plus women and children) from seven loaves of bread and a few small fish (Matthew 15:32-39; Mark 8:1-10).

The disciples gathered the leftovers from both events. They filled twelve baskets from the feeding of the 5,000 and seven from the feeding of the 4,000.

God used Elisha in a similarly miraculous way, although on a much smaller scale. One hundred men were fed from a knapsack of twenty barley loaves and newly ripened grain, with some left over (2 Kings 4:42-44).

The leftovers from the feeding of 5,000, 4,000, and 100 men in Elisha's time shows God's supply is always more than enough to meet our every need. The provision Christ makes for those who are His is not bare and scanty, but rich and plenteous; bread enough, and to spare; an overflowing fulness.[24]

After He was baptised in water and the Holy Spirit, the Spirit led Jesus into the wilderness to be tempted by the devil (Matthew chapter 4 and Luke chapter 4). The first temptation was to turn stones into bread.

This temptation seems straightforward. "Why don't you use your supernatural power to satisfy your hunger, as you have been fasting for forty days?"

---

24. *Matthew Henry's Commentary.*

Jesus refused to turn the stones into bread because of His faith in His Father to provide His needs. That's why He answered the devil by quoting an Old Testament scripture. He quoted only part of one verse.

If we read this verse in context, it reveals more than just the words Jesus quoted. The context is God testing the hearts of the Israelites during their time in the wilderness before they entered the promised land.

> And you shall remember that the LORD your God led you all the way these forty years in the wilderness, to humble you and test you, to know what was in your heart, whether you would keep His commandments or not. So He humbled you, allowed you to hunger, and fed you with manna which you did not know nor did your fathers know, that He might make you know that man shall not live by bread alone; *but man lives by every word that proceeds from the mouth of the LORD.* Your garments did not wear out on you, nor did your foot swell these forty years. (Deuteronomy 8:2–4, emphasis added)

This first temptation of the devil, as with all his temptations, was more than the actual words used, or reference quoted, always out of context. It involved Jesus fulfilling His needs, using His own ability, rather than trusting His Father to provide His needs.

If Jesus had provided for His needs using His own supernatural power, He would have failed to keep the commandments of His Father because of an unbelieving heart (according to Deuteronomy 8:2–4).

Therefore, if Jesus did turn the stones into bread, He would have destroyed God's plan of salvation for all of us because He would have died for *His sin*. He could not die for *our sin* after that. That's what the context of verse 3, which Jesus quoted, teaches us (the words I highlighted above).

Matthew tells us, "Then the devil left Him, and behold, angels came and ministered to Him" (Matthew 4:11). They supplied His needs.

> **Trusting God and His word is more important than having our immediate needs met.**

When we experience God's miraculous provision, our faith in Him and His word is always strengthened. Providing for our needs using our own strength or abilities, without acknowledging God as the ultimate source of our supply, exhibits a lack of faith in God. We miss God's provision and the opportunity to testify of the goodness and faithfulness of our God.

Jesus taught that He was the bread of life which came down from heaven (John 6:30–71). The Jews misunderstood, so they were offended by this teaching. Jesus was not saying they should eat His flesh or drink His blood; His teaching was that His coming death and resurrection would give life to all who received Him by faith.

The Feast of Unleavened Bread was part of the Passover ceremony instituted by God for the people to remember their miraculous deliverance from cruel slavery in Egypt (Exodus 12:1—13:10). Unleavened bread is bread made without yeast. In the preparation of household bread, a piece of fermented dough from an earlier baking was placed in the kneading trough along with fresh flour. This was then kneaded into cakes and then baked. Unleavened bread lacked the fermented dough.[25]

In teaching concerning the Feast of Unleavened Bread, Paul wrote "Get rid of the old yeast, so that you may be a new unleavened batch—as you really are. For Christ, our Passover lamb, has been sacrificed. Therefore let us keep the Festival, not with the old bread leavened with malice and wickedness, but with the unleavened bread of sincerity and truth" (1 Corinthians 5:7, 8, NIV).

Jesus taught his disciples that the leaven (or yeast in modern terminology) was the "deceptive teaching" (NLT) of the Pharisees and Sadducees (Matthew 16:8–12).

God expects us to live our lives trusting Him in sincerity and truth for all our needs. Trusting God for His provision must be more than just words. It must be demonstrated by our actions. We must live a life free from all hypocrisy, malice, or wickedness. Our lives should instead be characterised by integrity, sincerity, and truth.

---

25. *Encyclopedia of the Bible* (Author or date unknown).

Personal Application

- Do you acknowledge God's provision for your needs, or do you strive in your own abilities to supply your needs?

- Does God really supply your daily bread, even when you cannot see how this can occur?

- Can you believe for God's supernatural provision to supply all your personal needs? If you do, how do you react when you do not have enough to supply your or your family's needs?

- Can you share what you have with someone else, even if this is all that you have?

- Are you living a Christian life characterised by sincerity and truth, free of the hypocrisy of the Pharisees and Sadducees?

- What do you need to change in your life?

LESSON 10

First Human Reaction to a Crisis

Now it happened after these things that the son of the woman who owned the house became sick. And his sickness was so[26] serious that[27] there was no breath left in him. So she said to Elijah, "What have I to do with you, O man of God? Have you come to me to bring my sin to remembrance, and to kill my son?" (1 Kings 17:17, 18)

Everything was going along fine in our story. God miraculously fed Elijah, the widow, and her son every day. Then God sent or allowed a crisis.

When everything is going fine, a crisis comes. Sound familiar?

---

26. Severe (footnote in the NKJV Bible).
27. He died (footnote in the NKJV Bible).

This lady faced a crisis. Her young son died. The worst crisis is when you see your child or grandchild in pain and there is nothing you can physically do about it.

Most Bible commentaries suggest the widow's son did not die suddenly. Mathew Henry's commentary is a notable exception, as he suggests the boy died suddenly.

The direct English translation of the Hebrew words describing the widow's son in verse 17 reads "became ill and his sickness grew severe until no breath remained in him."[28] The NIV Bible uses the English words "He grew worse and worse, and finally stopped breathing" when describing the boy's condition.

The boy's sickness was not sudden or without warning. Elijah and the widow watched as the boy became sick, grew worse over a few days or perhaps a few weeks, and then died.

The widow's question to Elijah is translated in the NLT Bible, "O man of God, what have you done to me? Have you come here to point out my sins and kill my son?" (verse 18).

> **The widow blamed Elijah, and by extension God, for her son's death. This was all God's fault!**

The widow was really saying, "Why did you come here anyway? We would have been better off if we had never met you."

This was not a rational reaction. If you go back a couple of verses, you will read that if Elijah did not show up, the widow was ready to make one last meal then die because of

---

28. https://biblehub.com/text/1_kings/17-17.htm (accessed January 2024).

First Human Reaction to a Crisis

the famine caused by the drought. She and her son enjoyed two or more years of living in the blessing of God, which they would not have had if she had never met Elijah.

The widow's reaction is a typical human response to a crisis. Many people lash out at those around them when confronted with a crisis, just as the widow did to Elijah.

Lashing out does not solve the problem, it only alienates people. Sadly, a lot of people save the most heated words for those they are closest to, such as their loved ones, and often a close Christian friend, or the church leader or pastor.

The first reaction of many people to a crisis or when things do not work to plan is to blame God, the prophet, preacher, leader, or pastor for the problem.

How many times do we the same?

- Why did God allow my son to die?
- Why did God allow such a tragedy to happen?
- If He is a loving God, as you claim, then why does He allow so much suffering and pain or so much evil to continue in this world?

Elijah had learnt what to do in a crisis because he had already been in one. When the brook he was drinking from dried up, it was a crisis. He had learnt to trust God in that crisis, and now he was prepared for this crisis as well.

We need to learn the same lesson today, to trust God through a crisis in our lives because He has helped us through a previous crisis.

God always has a purpose for every crisis we face. When we face a crisis or when someone lashes out at us because of a crisis, we need to see the purpose God may have in this situation.

The devil and the world system tell us that tragedies and crises are all God's fault. Many insurance policies call such events an act of God. That is so wrong according to what I read in my Bible.

Bad things or crises happen to every human being because we live in a fallen world that is controlled by the prince of the power of the air—the devil himself (Ephesians 2:2).

A crisis is something in our lives that forces us, or at least provides us with the opportunity, to change, whether for good or bad.

> **The outcome of any crisis we face depends on our reaction to it, not on the crisis itself.**

One Friday afternoon, I was tired and late coming home from work (I had a full-time secular job as well as being the pastor of the church). I thought I would quickly race into the supermarket for a few small things.

Then, in an instant, I had accidentally locked my keys in the car. I had my mobile phone in my hand, so was able to ring the car service people (RACQ) to ask if they could help me retrieve my keys from my locked car. The answer was yes, but it might take more than an hour before someone would arrive there.

My first thought was, "Oh great, just what I need at this moment!" I was angry and fuming about how stupid I had been. What had I done today to deserve such a horrible, messy, frustrating situation? "God, why did you allow this happen?"

First Human Reaction to a Crisis

When I had cooled down, I felt the Holy Spirit reminding me that God had a purpose for this situation. I had to trust Him that He could use this for His glory. The reason this happened was so I could share God's love with the person who was coming to fix the car. I was able to share with the older guy who came in the service truck about who I was, who God was, and that God cared for me enough to make sure I did not lock my keys in the car in the middle of nowhere with no phone reception.

The privilege of sharing God's love and purpose with that older man was worth more than any crisis I had to go through first, even if this was my own fault.

I love the Bible stories, because I can read about real people in real situations to learn how they coped (or didn't cope) with a crisis in their lives.

Lot and his uncle Abram (who became Abraham in Genesis chapter 17) faced a crisis. They had to separate due to conflict between their herdsmen.

"But the land could not support both Abram and Lot with all their flocks and herds living so close together. So disputes broke out between the herdsmen of Abram and Lot" (Genesis 13:6, 7).

Lot chose to dwell in the land that was best able to support his livestock and possessions, despite how evil the people were (Genesis 13:11-13; 19:1-11).

Abram chose to stay in the land of Canaan and Hebron (Genesis 13:12, 18). This was hill or mountain country (Joshua 14:12, 13), and by inference not as well-suited for livestock grazing as the land that Lot chose.

Lot lived in Sodom. He was a righteous man who was tormented every day by seeing and hearing the wickedness of the men of Sodom (2 Peter 2:6-8).

God sent two angels into Sodom to destroy the city if they could not find ten righteous people (Genesis 18:20—19:11). Lot was faced with a crisis when the angels urged him to escape the coming destruction of the city (Genesis 19:12–22). He eventually chose to flee for his life, with only his wife and two daughters.

Lot lost all his livestock and possessions because he chose the best land for his livestock, despite the evil people who lived there, when he separated from Abram.

> When they were safely out of the city, one of the angels ordered, "Run for your lives! And don't look back or stop anywhere in the valley! Escape to the mountains, or you will be swept away!"
>
> "Oh no, my lord!" Lot begged. "You have been so gracious to me and saved my life, and you have shown such great kindness. But I cannot go to the mountains. Disaster would catch up to me there, and I would soon die. See, there is a small village nearby. Please let me go there instead; don't you see how small it is? Then my life will be saved."
>
> "All right," the angel said, "I will grant your request. I will not destroy the little village. *But hurry! Escape to it, for I can do nothing until you arrive there.*" (Genesis 19:17-22, NLT, emphasis added)

God would not destroy Sodom until Lot was safe. We must learn that God can keep us safe, even though we may suffer the loss of all or some of our material possessions by making the wrong choice in a crisis.

Moses faced a crisis. He killed an Egyptian who was cruelly beating one of the Hebrew slaves. Moses did this in

First Human Reaction to a Crisis

secret and in anger, but his murder was exposed. As a result, he fled from the palace and Pharaoh. He dwelt in the wilderness for the next forty years (Exodus chapters 2 and 3).

God had not forgotten Moses. He had a purpose for Moses existing in the wilderness for such a long time because of his own foolishness.

God said to Moses, "I will certainly be with you. And this shall be a sign to you that I have sent you: When you have brought the people out of Egypt, you shall serve God on this mountain" (Exodus 3:12).

The sign God gave Moses that He was with him was not the miracles or plagues God was going to inflict upon the Egyptians. It was that Moses would lead God's people, the Hebrew slaves, to serve (or worship) God on that mountain. In other words, God was telling Moses he was in the right place at the right time to do what He wanted him to do.

Moses learnt how to survive and look after sheep and goats during the forty years he was in the wilderness. He learnt where the water holes were, how to interpret the weather, and how to protect his animals from predators, especially at night. Without these survival skills, knowledge, and experiences, he could never have fulfilled God's plan for his life to lead the Hebrew slaves out of Egypt into that same wilderness.

When we feel we are in the wilderness, spiritually or physically, God has not forgotten you or me, even if we are there because of our own foolishness.

Notice in Exodus chapters 3 and 4, God never chastised Moses for murdering the Egyptian task master or fleeing the palace forty years earlier. God never chastises us for our sin or failings when we come to Him in repentance and ask His forgiveness through the blood of Jesus Christ (1 John 1:9).

Elijah's Victory, Part 1

King Jehoshaphat of Judah asked God questions when he confronted a crisis. A powerful army was coming against him that vastly outnumbered any army he could muster (2 Chronicles 20:1–12). Note verses 3 and 4, "And Jehoshaphat feared, and set[29] himself to seek the LORD, and proclaimed a fast throughout all Judah. So Judah gathered together to ask help from the LORD; and from all the cities of Judah they came to seek the LORD."

King Jehoshaphat sought his God, despite his fear of the crisis he was facing. He did not hide from his people the full extent of what they were facing. After commanding all the people to come to Jerusalem to face the crisis, King Jehoshaphat prayed, "O our God, will You not judge them? For we have no power against this great multitude that is coming against us; nor do we know what to do, but our eyes are upon You" (2 Chronicles 20:12).

God miraculously delivered him and his people because he sought God's deliverance in the crisis. He can deliver you and me from whatever crisis occurs in our lives, despite our fear, if we resolve to submit to His will in the crisis.

Luke describes a crisis in Paul's life in Acts chapter 27. Paul was a prisoner on a ship caught in a violent storm for fourteen days. He encouraged everyone on board the ship when he told them he had a vision from God that not one of them would lose their lives in the storm or shipwreck. The ship was wrecked on a sandbar and was broken in pieces by the pounding of the waves, but everyone on board was able to reach shore safely.

God has a purpose for every crisis we face, despite the circumstances of the crisis. He never leaves or forsakes us.

---

29. Lit. his face (footnote in the NKJV Bible).

First Human Reaction to a Crisis

When we know by faith that He is still in control, we *can* overcome any crisis we face.

There is one story of a crisis that God used to create the greatest revival recorded in the book of Acts. It is the story of seven sons of Sceva who tried to cast out an evil spirit from a demon-possessed man (Acts 19:11–20). That man overpowered these guys, who fled battered, bruised, and bleeding, with their clothes torn. God ensured everyone knew these seven brothers failed miserably trying to imitate the exceptional miracles God was doing through the apostle Paul.

As a result, the name of the Lord was magnified. Many believers who practiced black magic burned their books in a public bonfire. Those burned books were valued at 50,000 drachmas, or silver coins, which were each worth one day's wages for a worker.

The average weekly wage for an Australian working full time was $1,838 in August 2023.[30]

Assuming this is based on five days a week with no overtime, this is $300 a day (conservatively rounded figure). Multiplying 50,000 by $300 is equivalent to $15 million dollars' worth, in today's currency, of books on black magic, occult, witchcraft, astrology, spirit guides, or similar.

Can you imagine the result of such a public bonfire?

---

30. Results from Australian Bureau of Statistics, Earnings and working conditions. https://www.abs.gov.au/statistics/labour/earnings-and-working-conditions, accessed October 2023.

Personal Application

- Why do you believe bad things happen to good people?

- Can you explain this belief to someone facing a crisis to encourage them?

- Do you believe God can still use you for His purposes despite your failings in your Christian life? If you do, how does this belief help you when you face a crisis?

- Do you unconsciously or consciously blame God, the church, or the minister, when you face a crisis or when circumstances in your life just do not seem fair? If you do, what can you learn from this lesson?

- Do you react negatively to someone who blames God and/or you for a crisis in their lives? If you do, what can you learn from this lesson?

- How can you help someone in a crisis understand that God still has a purpose in their lives despite the circumstances?

LESSON 11

Second Human Reaction to a Crisis

Now it happened after these things that the son of the woman who owned the house became sick. And his sickness was so[31] serious that[32] there was no breath left in him. So she said to Elijah, "What have I to do with you, O man of God? Have you come to me to bring my sin to remembrance, and to kill my son?"
(1 Kings 17:17, 18)

A crisis has another effect—it brings us face to face with our sin, imperfections, and inward struggles.

Luke records a miraculous catch of fish after Peter (also known as Simon), his brother Andrew, James, and John had been on an all-night fishing trip (Luke chapter 5). They had caught nothing. There was nothing to

---

31. Severe (footnote in the NKJV Bible).
32. He died (footnote in the NKJV Bible).

show for their effort and nothing to feed their family or sell to others.

Jesus told Simon (and Andrew) to launch out into deeper water and throw their net(s) over the side of the boat one more time. When they did, they caught the largest number of fish they had ever caught in one go. They were, of course, overwhelmed by this event. "When Simon Peter saw it, he fell down at Jesus' knees, saying, 'Depart from me, for I am a sinful man, O Lord!' For he and all who were with him were astonished at the catch of fish which they had taken" (Luke 5:8, 9).

Fishing was all Peter and those who were with him had ever known. We know from other parts of the story of Peter's life as recorded in the Gospels that he was strong, brave, and self-reliant. Now he was confronted with a difficult or embarrassing situation he never expected. He was forced to admit that someone else, a religious man who was not a lifelong fisherman, knew more about fishing than he did. His life changed because of this event or crisis. Peter's reaction to his crisis was to recognise he was a sinful man, and this religious man was Lord.

Notice in the story that Jesus never mentioned sin or judgement directly to Peter. He may have listened to Jesus teach on this while He was sitting in Peter's boat (verse 3).

> **The second human reaction to a crisis is to be confronted with our sin.**

Many people in a crisis say or believe that they are being punished by God for their sin, or that God is

Second Human Reaction to a Crisis

reminding them of their sin even though they may have kept it hidden for a long time. That was also the reaction of the widow in Elijah's story (1 Kings 17:18), but keep in mind the following details:

- ❏ Elijah never confronted her about her sin.
- ❏ We do not know what her sin was.
- ❏ Elijah did not know what her sin was.
- ❏ The widow knew what her sin was.

Now she thought that God was judging her by allowing her only son to pass away. She was now believing the lie of the devil.

Both the widow in our story and Peter in Luke chapter 5 were confronted with their sin (whatever it was) when something happened that they could neither understand nor predict. They both faced a crisis.

Some people need to experience a crisis before they can be challenged to believe who God really is. God may allow a crisis to happen in the lives of those we pray for, to give them an opportunity to face their sin and need of His love and forgiveness. The crisis may be a crossroads in their lives where they must make a choice to accept or reject His love for them personally.

I believe we may need to change the way we pray for our friends, family, and those we are asked to pray for. Instead of asking God to keep them safe, we may need to ask God to do whatever is necessary, so this person is confronted with their sin and the saving power of our loving Lord Jesus Christ. That is more important in God's eyes than being kept safe from a crisis, or experiencing God's provision for their needs.

When I was twelve years old, I had some pet birds that I kept in a large cage on the verandah of our house. One morning, one of my pet birds escaped. I was faced with a crisis. My dad was not a great help, because he told me that my pet was either likely to die from starvation or cold or be eaten by the larger birds in our general area. Late that same afternoon, I rejoiced when I heard the familiar call of my pet bird, who was now sitting on the edge of our roof. Dad and I managed to coax that bird safely back into its special cage. I knew beyond any doubt that God loved and cared for me personally because of that crisis.

One year later, I attended a school camp in a rainforest area of a national park just west of Brisbane and the Gold Coast. We all walked for a swim in a large, deep pool of cold, clear water at the bottom of a tall waterfall. As we climbed over some large slippery rocks, I lost my footing and hit the back of my head as I fell into the rushing water.

All I remember was thinking the sharks were going to eat me, that I could not breathe, and I was bleeding as I was carried along by the strong current over the rocks. Then I remember deliberately thrusting my head above the water to take a breath.

When I finally opened my eyes and was conscious of what was happening around me, I was at the top of the waterfall with our nurse and ambulance people examining me to ensure I was OK.

Afterward, I heard the voice of God say to me, "Son, I saved your life from drowning." I prayed the sinner's prayer that night and gave my life to Jesus from that point forward.

Second Human Reaction to a Crisis

It is hard to help people in a crisis unless we truly know God's grace. "For by grace you have been saved through faith, and that not of yourselves; it is the gift of God, not of works, lest anyone should boast. For we are His workmanship, created in Christ Jesus for good works, which God prepared beforehand that we should walk in them" (Ephesians 2:8–10).

God's grace is never based on anything we may have done or not done, and nor is it about keeping religious rules or proving how holy we are by our actions. You should read Lesson 4 again for more information regarding God breaking religious rules.

The death and resurrection of Jesus Christ demonstrated God's love for all humanity. "But God demonstrates His own love toward us, in that while we were still sinners, Christ died for us" (Romans 5:8).

We must allow a person in a crisis to experience God's grace and forgiveness. His forgiveness is freely given to anyone who asks, no matter how bad or evil we may think someone's sinful acts have been.

I have had people say to me, "This crisis has come upon me because God is punishing me for my sin." I always try to say to these people (in confidence and diplomatically in love as best I can), "OK. What sin is God punishing you for? If you tell me God is punishing you, what is He punishing you for?" If the person (or persons) tell(s) me about a specific sin or event, then I remind them of God's forgiveness, grace, and that there is now no condemnation for those who are in Christ. As 1 John 1:9 states, "If we confess our sins, He is faithful and just to forgive us our sins and to cleanse us from all unrighteousness," and Romans 8:1, 2 reminds us, "There is therefore now no condemnation to those who are in Christ Jesus, who do not walk according to the flesh, but according to the Spirit. For the law of the Spirit of life in Christ Jesus has made me free from the law of sin and death."

I always try to challenge anyone who believes God is punishing them for sin to understand that God *forgives* them for sin; He does not *punish* them for their sin while they are alive on the planet. I also explain that they can experience God's forgiveness personally, with the true peace and freedom that only God offers them (read John 8:31, 32, 36; 14:27; 16:33).

As I am talking with such people, I always challenge the person(s) to accept Jesus Christ as their Saviour if they have not previously, or to recommit themselves to Him if needed. I always try to pray with and for them, using words such as "Lord Jesus please help this person or persons, to know your forgiveness, peace, and grace for…(I try to get them to name and confess their sin)"

When someone can't identify a sin they think God is punishing them for, all too often they answer with words such as, "Pastor, I don't know what I did, but I must have done something, and it must have been bad for all this to happen to me or my family."

My response to this statement is, "That sounds unfair for God to punish you when you do not know why. I know my God is never unfair."

Then I remind such people of God's love, protection, and blessing. I usually ask them to read the words to me from Psalm 91.

I always pray, either directly with them while they are talking to me, or afterward in my own quiet time. My prayer is that they may experience God's grace and love which is freely available to them and every human being on this planet.

Second Human Reaction to a Crisis

Many people who have a crisis will need more than just one short talk and prayer from me as a pastor. Follow-up times with these people are absolutely necessary until they can fully understand for themselves God's forgiveness, peace, and love.

Some people in a crisis may need professional help from suitably qualified people to overcome their crisis or associated feelings. Anyone who is counselling someone who is confronting or is in a crisis should always be aware of the need for professional referral. You should recommend this referral if, or when, needed.

God has shown me that when I minister to people in a crisis, I need to explain to them that God is still God despite what is happening to them or their family or loved ones.

People in a crisis are looking for confirmation of God's love, forgiveness of sin, and the knowledge that He is still looking after them even in their crisis. I believe God wants to provide this confirmation through us to everyone we may minister to.

Personal Application

- When faced with a crisis, do you believe God is judging you for your sin?

- Why or why not?

- Do you agree that sometimes we should ask God to do whatever He needs so that a person is confronted with their sin, instead of praying for God to protect them from a crisis?

- Why or why not?

- What can you learn from this lesson to help someone in a crisis to know that God loves them, has forgiven their sin, and is still guiding their lives?

LESSON 12

Honest Prayer

And he said to her, "Give me your son." So he took him out of her arms and carried him to the upper room where he was staying and laid him on his own bed. Then he cried out to the LORD and said, "O LORD my God, have You also brought tragedy on the widow with whom I lodge, by killing her son?" And he stretched himself out on the child three times, and cried out to the LORD and said, "O LORD my God, I pray, let this child's soul come back to him." Then the LORD heard the voice of Elijah; and the soul of the child came back to him, and he revived. (1 Kings 17:19-23)

Notice the words of the first part of Elijah's prayer, "O LORD my God, have You also brought tragedy on the widow with whom I lodge, by killing her son?" This is so important to our story. These words are not there by accident.

James chapter 5 tells us Elijah's prayer in this story was the best example of an effective prayer of a righteous man. We can learn from these words that we must pray honestly to God, not afraid to tell God how we feel about what or who we are praying for. His prayer, in my words, was:

- ❑ God, why did you allow this to happen?
- ❑ God, what are you doing in this crisis?
- ❑ Why did you mess up my plans? I almost had this widow believing in you because of the miraculous provision every day.
- ❑ Why did you have to let her son die?

God did not chastise Elijah for being honest in his prayer. He will never chastise or reject any person who prays honestly.

> **Praying honestly does not shock God.**

God already knows how we feel inside anyway. I am referring to our own private prayer and devotion time with God, not about praying in church or publicly.

In answer to Elijah's prayer, God performed a miracle. He raised the boy back to life. It was a miracle, I believe, because Elijah prayed honestly. He never hid from God how he felt about what had happened.

Many times I have asked, "How are you today?" In reply, I have received an answer about all the bad things that are happening to them or their family (often accompanied by why this is all God's fault).

Some Christian people respond to my question with "Well, praise God, I am pushing through by faith." That is true for many of these dear people. I praise God for them.

However, for others, these are just words as they struggle to build their faith with a positive confession despite the crisis. They cannot admit to God that they do not understand why He allowed this to happen, or where God is in the crisis.

These people can never confess to God their negative feelings, or their faith has been shaken by what has happened. They believe, or may have been taught, that to verbalise these reactions to their circumstances is a confession of unbelief or negativity, and is therefore disrespectful or doubting God. For them, such a doubtful confession is the opposite of confessing faith in God.

I have known dear Christian people facing a terrible crisis who have such an incredibly positive confession despite the situation. I could only marvel at their words of faith.

However, their positive confession was not based on faith at all. They believed if they keep positive enough for long enough God would reward them and do the very thing they were believing for. The motive for their words was to manipulate God to do what they wanted Him to do, instead of humbly trying to see how God could use this crisis for His glory.

I believe we need to tell God how we feel inside, then allow Him to lead us to pray despite our doubts and fears. We need to humbly ask God how He can change the situation so He is glorified by the outcome.

God never strikes us so we become a black spot on the floor because we dare to ask Him a question, or because we admit that we do not understand what He is doing.

In Luke chapter 1, the angel Gabriel came to Zechariah to prophesy the miraculous birth of John (who became John the Baptist) and to Mary to prophesy the miraculous birth of Jesus himself. Both Zechariah and Mary asked the angel a question.

"Zechariah asked the angel, 'How can I be sure of this? I am an old man and my wife is well along in years.'" (Luke 1:18, NIV).

"'How will this be,' Mary asked the angel, 'since I am a virgin?'" (Luke 1:34, NIV).

God did not judge Mary or Zechariah for asking a question.

Mary believed what the angel told her.

"'I am the Lord's servant,' Mary answered. *'May your word to me be fulfilled.'* Then the angel left her" (Luke 1:38, NIV, emphasis added).

God judged Zechariah because he did not believe what the angel told him. He did not trust God to miraculously change his circumstances so that God would be glorified.

"The angel said to him, 'I am Gabriel. I stand in the presence of God, and I have been sent to speak to you and to tell you this good news. And now you will be silent and not able to speak until the day this happens, *because you did not believe my words,* which will come true at their appointed time.'" (Luke 1:19, 20, NIV, emphasis added).

The difference between Zechariah and Mary was their reaction to what the angel Gabriel told them.

Jesus told a parable that turned the religious world of his time upside down. In Luke 18:9–14, He told the story of two men who went to the temple to pray. God answered the honest prayer from the heart of the despised tax collector and not the self-righteous prayer of the Pharisee or religious person.

Let us be honest with ourselves and God when we pray.

Honest Prayer

> **We do not need to be afraid to tell God how we feel, or how the situation looks from our perspective.**

We need God to show us what He wants to do when we are in a crisis. God can use any crisis to reveal His glory and power to people if we realise what He can do through it.

When I was visiting my dad, God said to me, "Tell your dad this will be the last time you see him, and he needs to get right with me."

This was hard for me to say, as my dad was very hostile to anything "religious" in his eyes. How was I going to say this to him? If I said this, I would be risking another angry outburst from Dad directed at me.

When we were drinking coffee at one of the coffee shops in a local shopping centre, I shared with him what God had told me. From past experiences, I did not know how Dad would react to me when I told him this. To my surprise, he didn't react as negatively as I had expected. He just ignored my words.

Seven months later, Dad passed away. I never saw him again, just as God had said. Mum told me later that Dad had finally accepted Jesus as his Saviour about three weeks before he passed away. I had said what God told me to, and God used this for His glory despite my fears about what might happen.

Elijah did something about the situation when the boy passed away.

He took the lifeless boy's body up to his room, then he prayed. Elijah allowed God into the crisis to perform such a wonderful miracle. Life returned to a lifeless body.

God's greatest miracle is to return spiritual life to a lifeless spiritual body.

Elijah physically stretched himself upon the child and in the second part of his prayer cried out to God for the child's soul to come back to him.

The first part of Elijah's prayer shows me he did not understand why the crisis came, but his actions and the second part of his prayer show me he still had faith in God. That is why he prayed for the soul of the boy to return. (Faith is believing without seeing, according to Hebrews 11:1.)

We must pray when we meet someone who is going through a crisis. People in a crisis need more than prayers with words such as "God bless you," or "God will work all things out for your good." These are ineffective prayers for someone in a crisis.

Be honest.

If you do not have the answers to why the crisis happened, why this person died tragically, or why they are facing a monetary crisis, health problem, or something else, you should not pray, act, or talk like you do have the answers.

I have found the best words to say to someone in a crisis are these or similar, "I do not know why this happened to you or your family; I do not have all the answers; but I do know my God, and He always has the answers. Would you like me to pray?"

If I do have a chance to pray, I include words such as "I do not know why this crisis happened. We (including the person or persons I am praying with) ask for wisdom, comfort, strength, peace, and help for the people in the crisis so that God may be glorified."

This event, this crisis, was also a significant test of Elijah's faith. Some of us may find it relatively easy to pray for

Honest Prayer

someone to be raised from the dead. We may have read about some great preacher praying and the dead person coming back to life. We can find books, biographies, or even YouTube videos or movies of a person who raised someone from the dead by the power of God, often in the most dramatic circumstances. Such stories are very, very inspiring. You should read or watch these if, and when, you have the opportunity.

However, Elijah did not have such stories to rely on. From what I can find in my Bible, God had never used anybody to pray and see the dead revived or come back to life before this event in 1 Kings chapter 17. We may think of Lazarus in the New Testament, in John chapter 11, who Jesus raised from the dead even though it was at least four days since he died, but that was many, many years after Elijah's time.

Elijah prayed the first part of his prayer, which was an honest prayer of "God, I do not know what to do about this." Then he prayed the second part of his prayer, as he trusted God to do something about the situation.

Does this sound familiar to anyone else?

Elijah's Victory, Part 1

Personal Application

- How does your faith in God prepare you for a future crisis, or sustain you in a current crisis or situation you cannot control?
- Can you pray honestly to God, telling Him how you feel in a crisis?
- Why or why not?
- Do you agree that a person with a positive confession despite a crisis could be just using words to try to manipulate God?
- Why or why not?
- What do you think is the difference between asking an honest question to God and expressing unbelief that God can answer your prayer?
- Do you believe God can use a crisis to reveal His glory and power to people?
- Why or why not?
- What can you learn in this lesson to help you pray for anyone in a crisis?

LESSON 13

Knowing God and His Blessings

And Elijah took the child and brought him down from the upper room into the house, and gave him to his mother. And Elijah said, "See, your son lives!" Then the woman said to Elijah, "Now by this I know that you are a man of God, and that the word of the LORD in your mouth is the truth."
(1 Kings 17:23, 24)

The miracle occurred; God restored her son to life. The widow now knew who the real God was. Isn't that exciting and a true testament of the faith of that lady?

However, we need to read this in the context of the story.

The widow was enjoying the benefits of daily food miraculously supplied for her, her son, and Elijah himself. She lived day by day with the benefits of acting on the words of Elijah, yet she still did not genuinely know God until her son was miraculously restored to life.

Elijah's Victory, Part 1

Too many people enjoy the blessings of God, sometimes for a long time, although they do not know God personally. They miss the relationship with God that they are desperately seeking, and that is a shame.

> **God is more than someone who is there to answer our prayers; He wants to have a relationship with each of us.**

Jesus Christ displayed the love of God for every human being on the planet when He died on the cross to set us free from the power of sin and the devil.

The story of Elijah in 1 Kings chapter 17 gives me an insight into a problem that I still have trouble understanding: How do people who see and experience the miraculous power of God in their lives, or in the lives of others, still not know who He is?

Why do some people walk away from or deny God after experiencing His miraculous power and blessings?

The reason, I believe, is because these people do not *know* God, or they treat Him just as a source of blessing.

It always amazes me when some people attend every church meeting and ask every person to pray for them when they do have a crisis. No trouble at all. However, when God does something about their crisis, they are there for a few weeks then I never see them again until the next crisis.

When we lived in tropical North Queensland, we experienced several cyclones (hurricanes or typhoons) in our time. There were some people who would be at every church meeting when the threat of a cyclone was there.

It was not hard to gather lots of people for a great prayer meeting when they were faced with a possible weather crisis.

Afterward, when it did not eventuate and the threat had passed, or it was not as bad as it could have been, some people would not come back to church meetings.

One of the hardest issues for me as a church pastor to accept is that some people will not come back to fellowship, church, or God when they receive an answer to their crisis. No matter how much effort and ministry I dedicate to allow God to fix their crisis, I will never see some people again.

Part of the issue, I believe, is because these people are only interested in God, church, or prayer activities so they can obtain an answer to their crisis.

The God of the Bible is more than just something or someone to get us out of our crises. He is the awesome, all-powerful God who created the world and all that we see in it today.

I have known people who pray prayers such as "God, if you do this for me or get me out of this crisis or bad situation, I promise I will never let you down and serve you for the rest of my life." God answers their prayer, often supernaturally, then they break their promise or bargain with God. They stay in the church family for a while, believing and trusting God (in their words anyway), before they leave and/or deny the very God they said they would serve.

Some people who have experienced the miracle-working power of God in their lives, or the lives of their friends or family, do not want to know God or understand His plan for their lives, because that is their choice. God respects their choice, even if it leads to their destruction. Despite this, God still longs for everyone on the planet to come to personally experience His love, mercy, and forgiveness.

The children of Israel, God's people, complained they had no new food after two months on their journey in the wilderness (Exodus 16:1–3). God supernaturally supplied food for them for the next forty years (Exodus 16:4–36) and water for them to drink (Exodus 15:22–26; 17:1–7).

Even though they collected God's food every morning (except the seventh day), they still complained (Numbers 11:1–15). Every time things got tough, they wanted to go back to Egypt. They refused to believe God would deliver them into the promised land because of the majority report of the spies (Numbers chapters 13 and 14).

They experienced the blessings and provision of God, yet still did not believe who He was or what He had promised He would do for them.

In Matthew chapter 23, seven times Jesus uses the words "Woe to you scribes and Pharisees," referring to their teaching and way of life, which was hypocritical and blind to God's grace and forgiveness.

Nicodemus recognised the miraculous power of Jesus Christ came from God. However, Nicodemus did not know God or understand what Jesus was teaching him about being born again (John 3:1–21). Jesus chastised Nicodemus for being a religious teacher of Israel without believing heavenly things.

In John 5:39, 40, Jesus rebukes the Jewish leaders, including the Pharisees and the teachers of the law: "You search the Scriptures because you think they give you eternal life. But the Scriptures point to me! Yet you refuse to come to me to receive this life" (NLT). The Jewish leaders chose to be blind to who Jesus was and refused to believe His words even though they witnessed many of his miraculous healings.

God has revealed his eternal nature and miraculous power through the created world, or the natural world, that so many people marvel at (Romans 1:18–32). Many people choose to worship the created things, rather than the Creator.

The children of Israel in the wilderness, Nicodemus, the scribes, Pharisees, and teachers of the law in Jesus's time, were all without excuse not to know who our God is. Everyone today older than their age of understanding is also without excuse.

My prayer for you from this lesson is that you may grow in your Chistian life as you learn to know God better, as Paul and Timothy prayed for the people in the church at Colossae:

> So we have not stopped praying for you since we first heard about you. We ask God to give you complete knowledge of his will and to give you spiritual wisdom and understanding. Then the way you live will always honor and please the Lord, and your lives will produce every kind of good fruit. All the while, you will grow as you learn to know God better and better.
>
> We also pray that you will be strengthened with all his glorious power so you will have all the endurance and patience you need. May you be filled with joy,[33] always thanking the Father. He has enabled you to share in the inheritance that belongs to his people who live in the light. For he has rescued us from the kingdom of darkness and transferred us into the Kingdom of his dear Son, who purchased

---

33. Or all the patience and endurance you need with joy (footnote in the NLT Bible).

our freedom.[34] and forgave our sins. (Colossians 1:9–14, NLT)

We should pray for God to give people "complete knowledge of his will"(NLT), or "to be filled with the knowledge of His will" (NIV), so that they gain spiritual wisdom and understanding.

You or I or those we pray for can only live to honour and please the Lord and produce good fruit in God's eyes when we have this spiritual wisdom and understanding. Only then can we know God better, learn to understand His ways in our lives, and have all the patience and endurance we need to live for God in our evil world.

This is how you and I can overcome the evil in our world today.

---

34. Some manuscripts add with his blood (footnote in the NLT Bible).

Personal Application

- Do you follow God only to get a blessing or an answer to your problems(s), or do you know who God really is?

- How can you have spiritual wisdom and understanding to know God's will for your life? (Read all of Colossians chapter 1 to help you answer this question).

- Do you know God's love for you, and do you experience this on an almost daily basis?

- What can you learn in this lesson to minister to people who come to church, experience God's miraculous answer to their prayer, then drift away from following God?

- Does your faith in God determine your actions, or do your actions determine your faith in God?

- Does your church need a "miracle (or healing) service" to attract people to continue to attend church?

- Why or why not?

A Final Word

Now that you have read this book and answered the questions in the Personal Application sections, I pray you will have gained a greater understanding that the lessons God taught Elijah are relevant to your life and ministry in the twenty-first century.

As you grow in your Christian life, may you minister to others who need a purpose and meaning in their everyday lives, just as Elijah ministered to the widow in his life.

May the words of this book be a positive part of your journey in preparation for wherever God may lead you in confronting the evil in your workplace, family, and neighborhood. You can only achieve this by the power of our God within you.

My prayer for you is that you will continue to grow into the Christian person God wants you to be.

My prayer for this nation is that Christian people will be so hungry for God to move in His supernatural power that our denominational beliefs, circumstances, or lives are not important anymore.

When Jesus delivered the Sermon on the Mount, recorded in Matthew chapters 5 to 7, His preaching was very different than that of the scribes because He taught as one having authority (Matthew 7:29). In the latter part of this sermon, Jesus taught us that entry into the kingdom of heaven has nothing to do with any works, including within church services, that we do for Him.

> Not everyone who says to Me, "Lord, Lord," shall enter the kingdom of heaven, but he who does the will of My Father in heaven. Many will say to Me in that day, "Lord, Lord, have we not prophesied in Your name, cast out demons in Your name, and done many wonders in Your name?" And then I will declare to them, "I never knew you; depart from Me, you who practice lawlessness!" (Matthew 7:21-23)

I believe in many churches the preachers or leaders miss asking people an important question based on Jesus's words in the Bible verses above. These churches have evangelistic meetings with the aim of presenting the claims of Jesus Christ to people. Often at such meetings, people are asked a very important question—"Do YOU know Jesus Christ as your Lord and Saviour?" This is the most important question anyone can ever be asked.

However, in many such meetings, a very important second question is often overlooked or neglected.

We must remember that we do great things for God, because we love God and want to reach people with the message of our Saviour's love for all humanity. Anything we do for God does not in any way guarantee our entry into heaven. That is only achieved by faith in Jesus's death and resurrection to cleanse us from all sin and enable us to live a life that pleases Him.

I must leave you with that second very important question at the end of this Bible teaching series:

Does Jesus Christ know YOU?

References

Barker, K. L. and Kohlenberger, J. R. III, (2004). *The Expositor's Bible Commentary (Abridged Edition): New Testament.* https://www.biblegateway.com/resources/The expositors-bible-commentary/toc/.

'*Billy Graham: An Extraordinary Journey—One ordinary man; One extraordinary God.*' TV Movie, Released March 4, 2018 (USA). Billy Graham Evangelistic Films; Virgil Films and Entertainment.

Carpenter, Wayne McCown (Editor, 1992), *Asbury Bible Commentary*, The Zondervan Corporation, Grand Rapids, Michigan, USA. https://www.biblegateway.com/resources/asbury-bible-commentary/toc/.

Encyclopedia of the Bible. (Author or date unknown). https://www.biblegateway.com/resources/Encyclopedia-of-the-Bible/toc/.

Hill, Stephen (1997) '*The Pursuit of Revival—Igniting a passionate hunger for more of God,*' Creation House, Strang's Communication Company, Lake Mary, Florida, USA.

Matthew Henry's Commentary on the whole Bible (referenced as *Matthew Henry's Commentary* in this book). https://biblehub.com/commentaries/mhc/.

Norwood, Arlisha, (2017). *Wilma Rudolph*, National Women's History Museum. Located at Alexandria, Virginia, USA. https://www.womenshistory.org/education-resources/biographies/wilma-rudolph.

Smith, William, (1863). *Bible Names Dictionary.* https://www.biblegateway.com/resources/smiths-bible-names-dictionary.

Other Books by Pastor James McClurg

What Is the Baptism with the Holy Spirit? (*2024*) This booklet (free to download from my website) provides biblical answers to all your questions about this topic.

A Mature Christian Leader (2022). This book provides hope to any Christian leader who has tried to grow in their Christian life, only to be disappointed with the results. Life qualities of mature Christian leaders (men or women) are introduced in this book. Each of the twenty-one life qualities is based on biblical principles and discussed in detail, with a Personal Application to allow the Holy Spirit to challenge you in your daily lifestyle

A Mature Christian Leader, Second Edition (Forthcoming). This soon-to-be-released book provides valuable new biblical insights into the life qualities of a mature Christian leader. Many practical examples are included in this updated version of how these life qualities should be displayed in the life of every Christian leader.

Is the Lord's Prayer Important for Us Today? (*in preparation*). This booklet will provide some important insights into the well-known prayer given to us as a model prayer. As we learn to apply the principles, rather than the words in isolation, we can grow in our Chrisitan life.

Elijah's Victory, Part 2: Overcoming Discouragement (in preparation). This book will provide biblical principles to help you overcome discouragement in your Christian life.

Lessons from the Kings of Israel and Judah (in preparation) Many Christian people do not read or understand the Old Testament history of the time when God's people (the Jews) were divided into the kingdoms of Israel and Judah. This book provides spiritual lessons derived from the historical and biblical details of this time. These lessons are relevant to our Christian lives in the twenty-first century.

Please visit my website for more information:
jamesmcclurg.com.au

About the Author

Pastor James McClurg has been a senior Christian minister for over thirty-five years in North Queensland, prior to semi-retiring in Bundaberg and then Sarina, Queensland, Australia. He has been married to Anthea for thirty-eight years and they have two sons and four grandchildren. Both James and Anthea are passionate about challenging Christians to live their lives according to the principles of God's Word—the Bible.

James and Anthea are excited to share practical lessons from the life of the prophet Elijah on how you can overcome the evil in your world in the twenty-first century. They love inspiring others to live victorious Christian lives by sharing their experiences and what God has taught them from the Bible. They always encourage anyone who listens to live a consistent, godly lifestyle.

They are both truly teachers and encouragers to anyone in the body of Christ.

www.ingramcontent.com/pod-product-compliance
Lightning Source LLC
Chambersburg PA
CBHW072337300426
44109CB00042B/1659